STRESS AND
RELAXATION

O P T I M A

STRESS AND RELAXATION

Self-help techniques for everyone

Jane Madders, Dip P Ed, M C S P

Consultant editor Michael Hay, M D, F R C G P

POSITIVE HEALTH GUIDE

© Jane Madders 1979

First published in the United Kingdom in 1979 by
Martin Dunitz Limited
Second edition 1980, third edition 1981, reprinted 1982, 1984,
1985, 1987

This edition published in 1988 by
Macdonald Optima, a division of
Macdonald & Co. (Publishers) Ltd
Reprinted 1990
Reprinted 1991

A member of Maxwell Macmillan Publishing Corporation plc

British Library Cataloguing in Publication Data

Madders, Jane
    Stress and relaxation – (Positive health
    guides)
    1. Relaxation
    I. Title   II. Series
    613.7'9

ISBN 0-356-14504-2

Macdonald & Co. (Publishers) Ltd
165 Great Dover Street
London SE1 4YA

Studio photographs by Simon Farrell

Photoset in Monophoto Garamond

Printed by Times Offset Pte Ltd, Singapore

SCIENCE

CONTENTS

ACKNOWLEDGEMENTS

My first debt is to all the people who have been in my relaxation classes: patients, students, teachers and men and women under stress who have helped me to modify my teaching to meet their needs.

I am particularly grateful to Dr Michael Hay for his interest and support over many years and for giving me the opportunity to work with his patients at the migraine clinic in Birmingham. He was also kind enough to read the manuscript and give me ideas and helpful criticism.

It is difficult to convey my appreciation of the hard work and dedication of the team involved in the production of this book but especially Martin and Ruth Dunitz, whose insight and high standards have been remarkable. Their personal involvement and enthusiasm have made my task an enjoyable one.

My thanks are due to the sympathetic photographers whose pictures illustrate this book: Simon Farrell, Arthur Burgess, Paul Blakey, George Kay, Mr R. Swift and Tim Fost; and to all the people who acted as models.

Finally, I must thank Max, my husband, who read each chapter as it was written and rewritten and managed to keep me calm and relaxed through the turbulent nine months before the book was born.

Jane Madders

The publishers would like to thank: Dunlop Sports Co Ltd for the photograph of the golfer on p. 38; IBM UK Ltd for the photograph of office equipment on p. 33; Ibbs & Tillet Ltd for the photograph of Eugene Sarbu on p. 61; G.P.A. Munich supplied the photograph on p. 85; Staples and Co Ltd for the bed on pp. 112, 113; the Nubian Lion (p. 111) is reproduced by courtesy of the Trustees of the British Museum; Steve Baruch for the photograph of the wedding reception on p. 107; British Airport Authority for photographs on pp. 117, 118; Zefa of London for the cover photograph.

Most of the modelling by Lynn Fitzgerald, Alan Borthwick, Wynne McGregor and Evelyne Duval.

FOREWORD

When I was a medical student we were taught about diseases. All too often, when there was no apparent cause for a number of symptoms, they were attributed to personal failure or to neurotic behaviour.

Thank goodness this attitude has changed as we have learned more about the way people need to adjust to their environment. Not only do we have a better understanding of what can happen when parts of the body begin to break down and no longer integrate well – but we are beginning to know how this may come about. It is similar to a car getting out of tune and leading eventually, if nothing is done about it, to a mechanical breakdown.

Everybody has problems to resolve and decisions to make. Our bodies are well adapted to recognize and respond to any situation which faces us. Arousal with accompanying tension is a healthy response but when excessive and prolonged it can cause ill health.

Shakespeare knew this when he put these words into the mouth of Macbeth:

'. . . why do I yield to that suggestion
whose horrid image doth unfix my hair
And make my seated heart knock at
my ribs against the use of nature?
Present fears are less than horrible imaginings.'

To some degree we all suffer from 'horrible imaginings' and the tension and unhappiness it brings. But we are not helpless; these reactions can be modified and controlled by training and that is what this book describes so well.

Jane Madders has long experience as a physiotherapist and teacher of health education and relaxation training, and has applied it in a number of contexts including childbirth, physical education and the alleviation and control of some common medical problems.

I have learnt a great deal at every one of her group relaxation sessions which I attended. There is always an atmosphere of informality, friendliness and humour, which enables the self-conscious to cast off their cares and to enjoy the programme of relaxation. Husbands and wives are invited to attend each other's final class so they can both understand the importance of relaxation at home and of daily practice.

Over twenty years I have referred hundreds of migraine sufferers to Jane Madders. Many of them were severely disabled by this common disorder which they tried to overcome by further effort and tension which could only make

9

things worse. Relaxation training has been of enormous benefit in teaching them how to prevent, or at any rate, alleviate their distressing attacks. Many patients have been able to discard pills altogether after attending a course of relaxation. This is reassuring when drugs so often treat the symptoms and not the cause.

All in all, Jane Madders's book is to be much welcomed and I feel sure it can only do good in today's world of unnecessary stress and tension.

K.M. Hay MBE, MD

INTRODUCTION

There is nothing wrong with stress and tension, they are necessary for success; but when they become excessive and prolonged, or our reaction to them is inappropriate, the body protests in various ways. This book shows you how to relax to counteract the ill effects of stress and fatigue.

Relaxation can be learnt by anyone and it can then be applied to daily living situations. It involves no drugs and there are no unpleasant side-effects, there are no difficult postures or strenuous exercise and it costs nothing. It requires some understanding of the basic principles, some practice and above all some confidence in the body's remarkable ability to heal itself and adjust to stress if only we give it a chance.

There are several reasons why it makes good sense to learn to relax:

It can be an effective way of coping with stress and the disorders it causes.

It can prevent or alleviate aches and pains caused by inappropriate muscle tension.

It can help to avoid unnecessary fatigue and is useful in aiding recovery after strenuous exercise.

It can raise the threshold of tolerance to pain.

It can enrich personal relationships because it is easier to get on with people when you are relaxed and at ease.

It can improve physical skills. The ability to avoid unnecessary muscle tension will improve performance whether you are a musician or a games' player and relaxation can lower excessive anxiety before a demanding event.

These claims are not wild ones based only on hopeful conjecture, they are all supported by research evidence from a number of countries as well as by more than forty years of my own professional experience.

It is important from the beginning to recognize that pain, fatigue and stress are warning signals. Pain and fatigue are important indications that the body requires some remedial action to be taken. Without pain, injured structures in the body would be further damaged by movement; without fatigue tired muscles and organs would continue working to exhaustion and destruction. Without arousal in response to a situation nothing would be achieved, no challenges met. The body has a wonderful integrating mechanism which enables all its systems to adapt quickly to changing situations and stress, whether these occur within it or in the external environment. When there is a threat to life the whole body goes into gear in preparation for vigorous activity. This 'Fight or Flight' reaction was appropriate for our primitive ancestors when faced with imminent physical danger but not for the stresses that our civilization brings. We react in the same way to over-crowding, frustrations of travel, the striving for status, rapid changes in life-style and problems of personal relationships. Our physical and chemical reactions to these stresses are often inappropriate, excessive and prolonged. There is plenty of evidence to show that these reactions can lead to a great many physical and mental disorders. Some of these are killers and others, while they do not destroy life, can seriously disrupt it and cause much distress and unhappiness.

Unfortunately, over the past few decades we have been promised instant tranquillity by an increasing number of drugs. In many countries there has been an unprecedented rise in the use of sleeping pills, tranquillizers, sedatives, alcohol and other mood-altering drugs. Now, doctors and the general public are becoming alarmed by the massive consumption of drugs, as well as by their side effects. Drugs are often taken to try to solve personal problems instead of facing up to them.

More people are looking for self-help natural methods to relieve tension. There has been a great rise in the number of enterprises which claim to lead to inner calm. Some of these are based upon sound principles, are well taught and give much help and support. Others, however, may become expensive and dangerous traps for those who are especially vulnerable when they are anxious, afraid and ill. Some of the bizarre remedies and therapies offered may add to their mental problems.

Voluntary control over internal physical conditions is not a new idea. Reports have filtered through over the centuries of the astonishing feats of yogis who were able to slow their heart beat, increase body temperature and influence other body functions not normally under voluntary control. It is only recently that there has been adequate research into the effectiveness of methods to acquire this control. Now there is ample evidence that relaxation techniques of several kinds can mark-

edly diminish the ill effects of prolonged anxiety and tension.

Perhaps this sounds almost too simple a concept, but anxiety and muscle tension go hand in hand. When you are alert and on guard the muscles tense for action. You can often see this in the habitual postures and gestures of yourself and other people: see the illustrations on pages 12 and 13.

Just as muscle tension is associated with arousal and anxiety, so relaxation can induce feelings of calm.

At first sight it may appear that this book is full of numerous exercises. Don't be put off by this. They are shown because a great many people are best helped by a dynamic approach, they want to 'do something about it'. Physical techniques have many advantages over purely mental ones and have added benefits. I have shown a number of different ways of recognizing muscle tension and relaxation, and exercises which help muscles to relax. Choose only those that suit you and discard the others. Only do as much as you feel capable of. Eventually you may not need the exercises except to keep mobile and enjoy movement. In the end, relaxation is not concerned with 'doing' but with feeling and with 'not doing', and daily practice of deep relaxation will become a habit. It can be practised anywhere, in a bus, a waiting room, at home, and partial relaxation will become absorbed into daily living. Those who wish to go on to meditation techniques will find that muscle relaxation enhances the experience, but many people will find the physical relaxation sufficient.

Half a century has gone by since, as a first-year student, I learnt to relax as part of physical education. We learnt it to improve physical skills and reduce fatigue but I now know that there is more to it than this. Since then I have taught relaxation to mothers before and after having their babies, to disturbed children and their mothers at a child guidance clinic, to students at a teacher training college and university and to many men and women attending the Birmingham Migraine Clinic.

I have gradually modified my teaching over the past forty years, changing as my class members and their physicians help me with their observations and by following up those who attended long afterwards. I shamelessly use parts of any methods which I find help them and myself. I have become increasingly aware, from experience and research evidence, that these techniques have additional and far-reaching effects.

Because this book is concerned with relaxation it does not mean that day-to-day exercise and diet are not important in coping with stress. Exercise, relaxation and nutrition are interdependent in maintaining good health.

It is unfortunate but understandable that the very people who most need to relax are those who are unable to accept the idea that there is something that they could do to relieve their distress. Sometimes they are afraid of what might happen if they let go of tension. They may be helped by the kind of massage I illustrate. These are simple techniques which could be used by a partner to provide a pleasant first step towards relaxation.

Most of the following chapters begin with some factual information for those who like to have an explanation underlying their practice. You can skip this if you prefer and go on to the illustrated practical suggestions.

Signs of tension

Many people are tense without even realizing it. As you are reading this it is quite possible that you are working very hard even though you are just sitting. Your shoulders may be tight and hunched, or your teeth clenched and jaw jutting forward. There are many different ways of showing tension and some of them are illustrated here.

Hair twirling

Ankle bending or tapping

Coiled legs

Arms folded tightly, abdomen drawn in

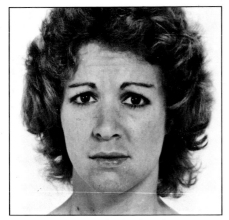

Worry muscles of the forehead are contracted

Nail biting

Tight, hunched shoulders

Clenched teeth and a jutting jaw

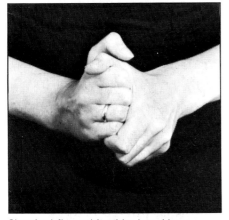

Clenched fists with white knuckles

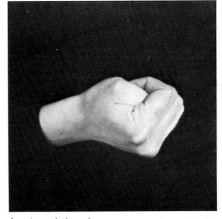

A gripped thumb

15

1 STRESS

What is stress?

The interpretation of what is stressful and the reaction to a source of stress will be different for each of us. The way we react will depend upon our vulnerability: the result of our genetic make-up, childhood experiences and environment. Most people have a tendency towards using one pattern of bodily reaction rather than others, for example, some have stomach upsets, others headaches, respiratory illness or high blood pressure. Several members of any one family often show a similar pattern.

Some people thrive on stress; they are the ones who get a thrill out of climbing mountains, sailing in rough conditions, or politics. To them it is the spice of life and many of us enjoy the heady excitement of being a little nervous. Others are more sensitive and crumple at mild criticism; some simply don't notice it. Too little stimulation brings flatness and depression; too much can lead to anxiety, panic and illness. But throughout life, stress is unavoidable and a certain level of arousal is necessary for effective performance at work.

So what is stress? To clarify what I mean by the term, it is helpful to look at some of our current usages of the word in different fields.

We have borrowed the word 'stress' from physics and mechanics where it means the physical pressure exerted upon, and between, parts of a body; when deformation occurs as a result it is called 'strain'. It is easy to see how we use these terms when we refer to 'the stresses and strains of life' meaning something which distorts our comfortable way of living.

In common language 'stress' is associated with distress, meaning any kind of burden, pressure or hardship. 'The stress of modern living' usually means any conditions that give rise to worry, tension and frustration.

In biological terms stress means anything constituting a threat, real or apparent, which would adversely affect the organism.

None of these definitions enfolds the whole concept of stress as it applies to the human condition. The broad view described by an international authority on stress, the physiologist Dr Hans Selye, in his book, *The Stress of Life*, goes beyond these. He defines stress as 'the rate of wear and tear of the body' and showed that there is a generalized adaptive response to stress whether the agent we face is pleasant or unpleasant. Cold, heat, rage, drugs, excitement, pain, hormones, grief, even sheer joy, all elicit the stress mechanisms of the body *in the same way*.

Because of the difficulty of defining stress it is becoming customary to talk of 'arousal' instead. 'Arouse' means 'to stir up' and this describes very well the way the body prepares itself for action. Adaptability is probably the most distinctive characteristic of life and arousal stirs up the body to adapt to anything that appears to be a threat to survival. 'Appears' is the word I have chosen because the body is not always wise and can produce stress reactions to situations that are not a real threat to life. Claude Bernard, a nineteenth-century French physiologist, was one of the first to see disease as the outcome of attempts at adaptation, appropriate in kind but faulty in amount. Walter Cannon, the famous Harvard physiologist, in his book, *The Wisdom of the Body*, called the power to maintain equilibrium 'homeostasis'. He showed how this leads the body to enable it, in a remarkable way, to prepare for 'fight or flight' whenever it is threatened.

The fight or flight reaction

As soon as danger is recognized, the muscles immediately tense for action, ready to fight or run away. They tense like a sprinter waiting for the signal to go. This is a reflex action which shortcuts the brain because it has to be instant (remember this muscle tension when we come to consider how relaxation can diminish the alarm reaction). The message of danger is received by the brain and dramatic changes are then initiated by the hypothalamus. This is the remarkable centre which integrates all the functions of the body which are not normally under our conscious control.

The hypothalamus co-ordinates all the different activities of the body. It is situated just above the pituitary gland which is often referred to as the leader of the endocrine gland orchestra because it stimulates all the other glands into action. The message is passed on by the hypothalamus to the pituitary and, by means of hormones, the body is then alerted for action to prepare it for vigorous physical activity. Every part of the body is involved. It is all under the control of the sympathetic nervous system which is responsible for action to meet possible danger, and the parasympathetic which is concerned with restoring the body to peaceful activity after an emergency.

In a fight or flight reaction the muscles, heart, lungs and brain have priority and all other systems have to take second place in the emergency.

How the body prepares for fight or flight

In order for the muscles to work effectively they require fuel in the form of glucose so the liver releases some of its store of blood sugar and it is carried to the muscles in the bloodstream. Oxygen is also needed to transform the glucose into energy so this also is carried by the blood. Therefore, the heart has to pump harder to get the blood where it is most needed and blood pressure rises as a result.

There is a limit to the amount of blood available in the body so it has to be diverted from somewhere else for the time being. Digestion slows down or is halted; the salivary glands dry up; the stomach and intestines stop working and the sphincter muscles close to avoid defaecation and urination taking place (sometimes the parasympathetic nervous system over-reacts and the opposite occurs with 'wetting your pants with fright' and diarrhoea). The blood vessels in the kidneys constrict. Because the lungs must take in more air to provide oxygen and must also get rid of more carbon dioxide, breathing must become faster, deeper or gasping. The adrenal glands secrete adrenalin and other hormones to keep the fight or flight reaction going. The usual anti-inflammatory mechanism which deals with infections in the body would be a nuisance in battle so it is subdued (infectious illnesses are more likely to be caught when we have been under stress for some time).

Even the skin changes under stress.

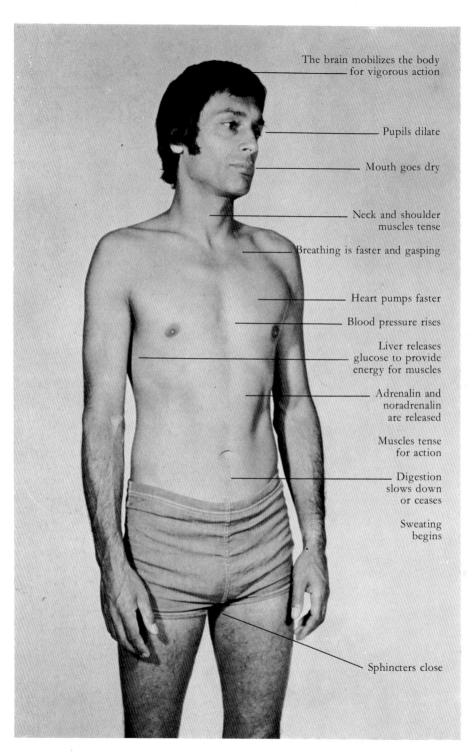

The brain mobilizes the body for vigorous action

Pupils dilate

Mouth goes dry

Neck and shoulder muscles tense

Breathing is faster and gasping

Heart pumps faster

Blood pressure rises

Liver releases glucose to provide energy for muscles

Adrenalin and noradrenalin are released

Muscles tense for action

Digestion slows down or ceases

Sweating begins

Sphincters close

How the body prepares for fight or flight

If these reactions are prolonged they can lead to the disorders shown on page 20.

Because the body is likely to get overheated in vigorous activity the skin prepares for cooling by sweating, and the electrical resistance of the skin is lowered. In order that some of the blood may be diverted to muscles the capillary blood vessels constrict and we may look pale as a result. The skin also has to excrete more of the body's waste products.

There is a change in the chemical composition of the blood with more salt and less potassium. The pupils of the eyes dilate.

All these, and many other complex changes occur, some of them in a split second. When physical action has been taken and the danger is over, the biochemicals of stress used up as intended, everything settles down to normal, relaxation takes place and no harm is done. The body has adapted to normal stress and equilibrium is once more established.

The effects of prolonged stress

It is when these normal and useful reactions are prolonged, excessive and inappropriate that the trouble begins. The fight or flight response is important for all animals when life is threatened, but we are unlike them in that we can produce these physical and chemical changes for situations that do not require vigorous physical activity. A car driver fuming at traffic delays, a mother exasperated by her children, frustrating committee meetings, being late for an appointment, a row with the boss, an income tax demand, may all produce the same response as those for a threat to life.

For example, it was shown that while the pulse rate of someone doing physical work was 145 beats a minute, the rate for an interpreter doing simul-

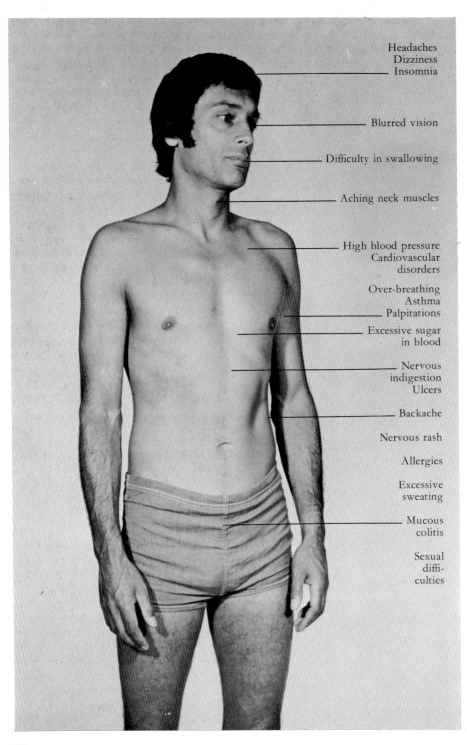

Headaches
Dizziness
Insomnia

Blurred vision

Difficulty in swallowing

Aching neck muscles

High blood pressure
Cardiovascular
disorders

Over-breathing
Asthma
Palpitations

Excessive sugar
in blood

Nervous
indigestion
Ulcers

Backache

Nervous rash

Allergies

Excessive
sweating

Mucous
colitis

Sexual
diffi-
culties

Some disorders related to stress

Although these disorders may be the result of reaction to prolonged stress there might be other causes which require medical help.

taneous interpretation was as high as 160. Someone doing addition at the rate of forty one-digit numbers a minute more than doubled his adrenalin output. These people were responding as though they were doing battle when they were sitting still in a chair.

Our highly developed forebrain also enables us to dwell on past events or imagine future ones and maintain all the circulating stress biochemicals. So instead of the reactions being adaptive short-lived ones, they persist over very long periods. It is now known that emotional states, when they continue for a long time, can have profound effects on the body, sometimes damaging the organs, sometimes predisposing them to infection.

Stress disorders

If you look back to page 18 and imagine these changes persisting over a long time you will be able to understand how stress plays a part in many disorders. For example, if blood pressure remains high and blood vessels constricted, there may be cardiovascular disease in the form of heart attacks or strokes. If the stomach remains with its impoverished blood supply and the mucous membrane of the gut engorges there will be digestive disorders such as duodenal or stomach ulcers, mucous colitis, constipation or diarrhoea. If the lungs continue to strive for more air there will be over-breathing with associated giddiness and fainting, or it may add to the problems of asthma. The skin changes may lead to allergies and rashes for those who have such a tendency. Where muscle tensions are sustained there may be headache, backache and aches and pains in the muscles, especially in the neck and shoulders.

If the anti-inflammatory mechanism is subdued for long there will be a

21

greater susceptibility to infections of various sorts. The Common Cold Research Unit in Salisbury, England, recently found that anxiety had a marked effect on the chances of volunteers catching a cold. It has also been observed that apparently unrelated illnesses, including infections, seem to come in clusters following times of stress. High levels of arousal have also been found to lower fertility by hormone changes and also contribute to some menstrual disorders. Long-term anxiety may also bring feelings of panic which seem to have no reason but which can be frightening and crippling.

It is, of course, important to note that stress is not the only factor involved in these disorders, nor is it necessarily the main one, but there is now plenty of evidence to show that it may play a significant part in promoting, or triggering off, a great many illnesses.

Some causes of over-arousal

Dr Peter Nixon, Senior Consultant Cardiologist at Charing Cross Hospital, London, has found contributory causes for sustained and inappropriate high levels of arousal. His findings were mainly in the field of cardiovascular disease, but have universal implications.

1. 'People poisoning' (pressures exerted by people from whom there is no escape)
2. Unacceptable time pressures
3. Sleep deprivation
4. A high score in life-style changes

This latter has been a subject of study in the USA by Professor Holmes and his colleague, Dr R. Rahe.

The effects of life-style changes

It was found that four out of every five people who experience many dramatic changes in their lives can expect a major illness within the next two years. Dr Rahe quantified forty-three life-style changes, using a major change such as the death of a spouse for a score of 100, and marriage as fifty. Some of the typical changes are listed below:

Death of a spouse	100
Divorce	73
Personal injury or illness	53
Fired at work	47
Retirement	45
Sex difficulties	39
Gain of a new family member	39
Change in responsibilities in work	29
Outstanding personal achievement	29
Change in living conditions	25
Change in work hours or conditions	20
Change in sleeping habits	16
Change in eating habits	15
Christmas	12
Minor violations of the law	11

This is not the complete list and some points will not be relevant to everyone; your own list might be different. It was found that when the score (using the full forty-three items) was over 300 there was likely to be serious illness, while a score of over 100 indicates that remedial measures to limit the reaction to change should be taken.

People react differently and it is not the situation itself that produces illness, it is the continual arousal that causes the trouble. It is wise, therefore, for us to avoid having more than one major change at a time. For example, if you are about to retire, it is better not to move house at the same time; get one change over with first; if you take on a new job it will not be the best time to start slimming and getting married all at once. We need to space our changes as much as we can, but if we have to meet several major changes simultaneously we can adjust our reaction to them and relax, thereby lowering the level of arousal.

Arousal is necessary

An optimum level of arousal is necessary for achievement but too much impairs performance and leads to exhaustion and illness. Dr Nixon has devised a Human Function Curve which plots a comparable curve of performance against arousal. The following descriptions will help you to assess your own level of stress.

Where do you stand on the curve?
Healthy tension You feel well, your manner is relaxed and physical

Human function curve

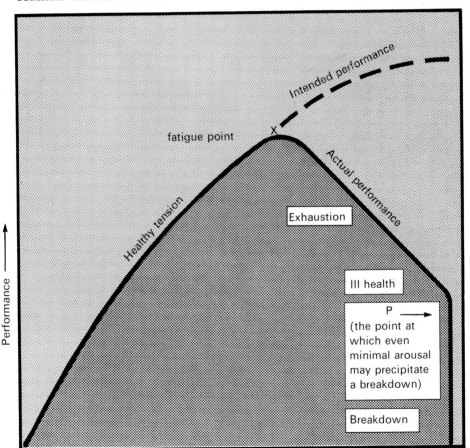

When fatigue point X is reached, the harder the person tries the less he achieves. If the arousal continues at a high level it can lead to exhaustion, ill health and eventually breakdown. Relaxation techniques can reduce fatigue and raise the level of performance.

recreation brings pleasure. You don't feel guilty at taking time to relax or take exercise. Burdens and pressures that would cause loss of happiness and health are rejected. Other people see you as healthy, adaptable and approachable. The qualities required for success, namely rapid and flexible thought, originality, vigour and capacity for sustained effort, are abundant. Increasing your arousal improves your performance.

Acceptable fatigue You may feel reasonable fatigue but don't deny it and take steps to recover as soon as possible. Inessential drains on energy can be jettisoned or deferred (one of my jobs when I taught relaxation was to teach people how to let other people down sometimes). Sleep is adequate, other people see you as healthily tired, but they are not made anxious about it. The qualities required for success are still evident.

Exhaustion You may insist that you are healthy but other people see differently. You see no need for relaxation, nor to increase fitness. Excessive burdens and pressures disruptive of health and happiness are accepted as inevitable because exhaustion reduces the ability to distinguish the essential from the inessential. You may engage in fruitless activity (we often see this in exhausted mothers who take on more and more and in colleagues in whom the 'martyr syndrome' is easily recognized by others). Increasing the arousal only worsens the performance and this makes for more anxiety and greater arousal.

Others see the signs of strain: bad temper, grumbling, longer hours worked but less achieved. There may be preoccupation with minor matters while major problems wait to be solved. Sleep becomes inadequate and

mannerisms may develop which disrupt the peace of mind of others. The qualities for success disappear and the mind becomes set against change; adaptability is lost. Eating, drinking and smoking may increase or the appetite is lost and meals are skipped. The more seriously exhausted you are the less likely it is that you will seek medical help. If this stage continues it leads to ill health and eventually it requires only a minor irritation ('P' on the curve) to precipitate a breakdown in mental or physical health. Most of us have either experienced these feelings or watched someone else experience them.

What can we do about it?

It would be presumptuous for me to offer advice for situations which are intolerable and where only help by counsellors or friends will tide over the crisis. There are, however, ways of diminishing the effects of stress if you take a long look at yourself and take action before cracking point.

1. Know yourself and how much arousal you can tolerate. Have the courage to say 'no' when things are too much. Recognize fatigue and take action to remedy it. Take time out, and 'box clever'.
2. Change the environment. Get away from the situation that causes the stress. This may mean changing your job, moving house, leaving home. This may be impossible, and in any case may not solve the real problem.
3. Habituation. Get used to it by facing the stressful situation frequently.
4. Keep fit. When you are well and healthy, when nutrition, exercise

and sleep are adequate, it is much easier to cope with stress.

5. Hobbies and leisure pursuits are distractions and take the mind off immediate problems. Creative use of leisure time is important.

6. Accept the feelings of stress and don't let them alarm you. Later on, use the experience to deepen your understanding of other people.

7. Help others. Man is a social animal and needs the support of others. If we can earn and receive the gratitude of other people, and equally important are able to show gratitude to them, we can share problems and cope with stress without distress. This is 'The Philosophy of Gratitude' propounded by Hans Selye.

8. Learn to lower the level of arousal. Psychologists and physiologists have shown that a state of muscle relaxation is incompatible with that of anxiety. It is muscle tension which first signals 'Danger' to the brain. By relaxing muscles the message is received that all is well. Muscle relaxation can be an effective way of lowering arousal.

2 MUSCLE TENSION, POSTURE AND FATIGUE

Muscle tension and fatigue

Activity is essential to life. If human beings stay in one position for a long time, they experience pain and fatigue whether the cause is physical or emotional. Muscles benefit from movement and they need the good circulation of the blood that follows. Movement directly induces relaxation because muscles work in pairs, one group relaxing as the opposing group

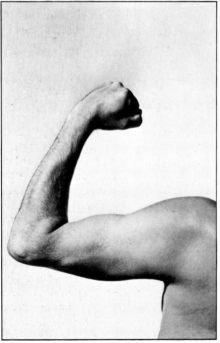

When one group of muscles contracts, the opposite group relaxes.

contract. This can be seen and felt if you bend your arm at the elbow.

When the biceps muscle in front contracts, the triceps muscle at the back relaxes at the same time to allow movement to take place. When the arm is straightened out the triceps contracts and the biceps muscle relaxes. In all movement, therefore, there is an in-built relaxation of muscle which aids circulation and the removal of waste products.

If muscles are held tight and tense in static contraction for long periods, however, the circulation is impeded and there will be a build-up of fatigue products. This can cause the muscle to go into cramp-like spasm, causing the aches and pains so familiar to many tense, over-alert people. This especially applies to the muscles of the neck and shoulders. Sustained muscle tension can have other harmful effects. Even holding a fist clenched for a while can significantly raise blood pressure.

Much sustained muscle tension goes unnoticed. It is possible that, as you are reading this, you may be physically working very hard. Your shoulders may be held tight, your jaw clenched, your legs held tightly together or you may be adopting one of the tense postures illustrated in the introductory chapter. This prolonged tension will cause you to be more tired at the end of the day than you should be and you may have muscular aches, perhaps headache, backache, tender places in your shoulders and neck as a

26

result of tension. Continual tension of the jaw with teeth clenched tightly together is a common cause of tension headaches as well as dental disorders.

Why muscles ache

There are about 620 skeletal muscles in the body. These are the ones which move limbs and spine and produce movement. They are also called voluntary muscles because, unlike the muscles of the blood vessels and internal organs such as the stomach and heart, we can exert conscious, voluntary control over them. Skeletal muscles are made up of bundles of parallel fibres and these are enclosed in a strong membrane. The bulge in the middle of a muscle is where the number of fibres is greatest. Each fibre is composed of a large number of slim filaments which can contract and expand like elastic. When thousands of these work together the muscle contracts.

For a voluntary movement to take place, a message from the brain travels along nerves to the muscles required to work, then the end of the nerve releases a chemical which almost instantaneously sets off a chain of reactions which will lead to a release of energy. Only part of this chemical energy is converted into activity, the rest is generated as heat. The process involves the chemical breakdown of glycogen, a form of sugar, in the presence of oxygen, both of which are transported to the muscles by the bloodstream. So the maintenance of good circulation is necessary for muscle action.

In addition to heat being generated, the breakdown of glycogen produces fatigue products, mainly lactic acid. This is cleared away in the bloodsteam, particularly in the relaxation phase of the movement. When the circulation is impeded by prolonged contraction of muscles, however, there will be an accumulation of lactic acid and it is this that leads to pain, stiffness and physical fatigue. This is understandable and acceptable when it is the result of strenuous activity but is unnecessary when it is the result of poor use of the muscles. Good circulation and muscle relaxation are therefore necessary to reduce the effects of lactic acid in the muscles.

Intermittent tension does no harm at all; it is the small continuous abuses that do the greatest damage. Rhythmical exercise, by the alternate contraction and relaxation of muscles, will improve circulation and avoid or mitigate the pain and fatigue caused by muscle tension. You can probably remember times when you felt too tired to go out in the evening but, after a night of dancing, the backache and tiredness had gone and you felt refreshed. This was not just the result of enjoying yourself but also the effect of rhythmical activity assisting muscle relaxation.

Recognizing muscle tension

Before you can learn to relax you must first be able to recognize tension. I have seen many classes where members were told to relax, and they and the class teacher believed they had been successful when, in fact, their muscles were still tense. Some people have acquired a habit of muscle tension over a great many years and are so accustomed to it that they are unaware of inappropriate contraction of muscles. It is no use *telling* such people to relax; they are quite unaware they are tense or what it feels like to be relaxed. Knowledge is required about the state of the muscles and there are several methods of getting this.

Recognizing tension by touch

The most natural and also one of the most effective methods of assessing muscle tension and relaxation is by touch, by actually feeling the difference between tense, contracted muscle and a soft resting one, either on yourself or on other people. You can feel the varying degrees of muscle tension in your arm in the following way.

Reach across with one hand and take hold of the top of your upper arm. Raise that arm a little and make the whole of it tight and tense. You will feel the muscle go tight and hard. Feel all over the arm. Then let the arm rest by your side and feel the difference: the muscles are soft and you can get hold of handfuls of flesh. Now do this again but without actually moving the arm, just *prepare* to lift it. As you do this you will feel a differing degree of tension. This is the sort of contraction you make when you are on the alert and ready for action. Release the tension and feel the contrast. You will notice that, when it is soft and relaxed, your shoulder has dropped also and is no longer held tightly.

Feeling tension in hands

Grasp one wrist with the other hand. Grip it tightly so that your muscles show white and you are actually holding up the underneath hand. Feel the strength of this grip on your resting hand. Now release the tension and feel the difference: the fingers on the top hand are feather-light and the underneath hand is giving all the support.

Try to notice when you hold your hands tight during the day, and notice other people too.

Tension in neck muscles

Feel the muscles at the back of your neck by taking hold of them as though you were picking a cat up by the scruff of its neck. If your head is resting easily the muscles are soft. Keep hold and slowly jut your head forward to the tense position. You will feel the muscles go tight and hard under your hand. You can sometimes see tramlines of tension in these muscles.

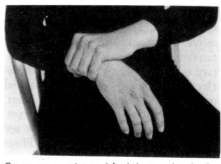

Grasp your wrist and feel the tension in the top hand.

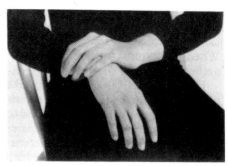

The relaxed top hand is soft and rests upon the other.

28

For the arm to lift, the muscles must contract and feel hard.

In a relaxed, resting arm the muscles are soft.

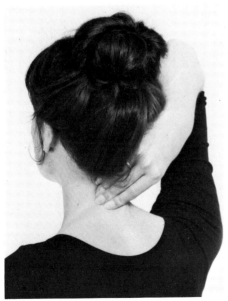

When sitting, or standing upright, the neck muscles should be relaxed.

Bend the neck forward and feel the muscles tense.

Partner lifts an arm by supporting the elbow with one hand and the wrist with the other. Arm should feel heavy and limp.

When partner removes the support, the arm should drop immediately and loosely because it is relaxed.

Testing relaxation with a partner

Try this out on your friends and see whether they can relax arm muscles.

Place one hand under the wrist and the other under the elbow. Lift the arm and if it is relaxed it will feel heavy and limp. You will be able to move it easily because your partner neither helps nor hinders the movement. If you let go it will immediately drop to the side. Some people will resist the movement or tighten up to offer the arm to you. Others really relax and you can tell this at once. (This does not necessarily mean that they can apply relaxation to daily living, but they do understand how to relax muscle at will.)

By testing this way, even if your partner cannot relax, it gives you a good idea of what tension and relaxation feels like, and also of the wide variety of individual differences be-

tween people. It is also useful as a way of assessing progress, but remember that even a little degree of improvement helps relaxation and there is no need to despair if you are not good at relaxing when a partner tests you.

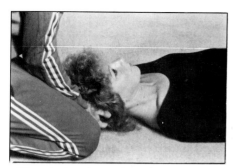

Lifting the head – neck tendons are clearly visible.

Lifting the head – neck muscles relaxed, no tendons visible.

Partner testing relaxation in neck muscles

Kneel behind your partner who lies on her back with knees bent. Cup your hands under the head and lift it *very gently* just a little way. Feel the weight of it (somewhere between 12–14 lb or 5–6 kg). If the neck muscles are relaxed, the head offers no resistance. If the muscles are tense you can see the tendons standing out as the muscles lift the head.

Learning by observation

Another way of recognizing tension is to observe movement in other people. Watch dancers, golfers, gymnasts, musicians, even someone beating an egg or driving a car and spot the tense and relaxed phases of the movement. Grace and ease of movement are the result of economy of effort with muscles contracting only when they are needed. Look out for tension in other people and notice tight shoulders, neck, ankles. Some people remain tense when they are asleep.

Learning by contrasting contraction and relaxation of muscles

This is the method which originated from the work of Edmund Jacobsen in the United States and was described in his book, *Progressive Relaxation.* It is favoured by clinical psychologists, behavioural therapists and many relaxation teachers. It involves a systemic routine of contracting strongly each group of muscles of the body in turn and then releasing the tension. All parts of the body are involved and learning and practice takes a long time. These strong contractions certainly help many people to recognize the difference between tension and relaxation but there is now evidence that some anxious people find it difficult to dissipate the tension and are actually

31

more tense afterwards.

Most people react to stress by adopting the readiness-for-action posture involving flexion of the muscles, for example, by bending the ankle upwards, or shoulder hunching. Individuals are different, however, and there are some people who do not adopt the characteristic fear response with postural flexion when they are alarmed, but do the opposite, they stiffen and straighten. Dentists say that frightened patients often stretch out their fingers instead of clenching them. So it is wise to recognize that no method of relaxation is unique; each builds on the work of others, and there are many different ways of reaching the same end.

Biofeedback

There are feedback systems in all living organisms. The methods of recognizing muscle tension I have described in

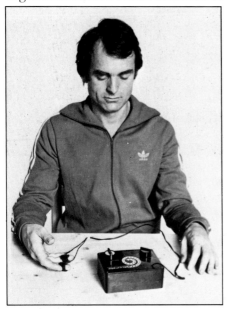

Using a biofeedback machine.

this book involve ways of feeding back information to the user about what muscles are doing. 'Biofeedback' is the term used to describe the use of electrical instruments which, when attached to the user, *feed back* an audible or visual signal about a particular function (one which is normally not under voluntary control) so that he can learn to exert some control over it. It includes apparatus to help the learner to modify his muscle tension (usually in small groups of muscles), brain waves, body temperature, skin resistance and other functions. Biofeedback machines are *teaching aids*; in themselves they do nothing to the user and do not cause the change. They help him to learn or re-learn control of physiological functions and they monitor his success or failure.

The electromyophone gives information about muscle tension but it is the battery-operated skin resistance galvonometer, which indicates changes in levels of arousal, that I have found most helpful as a teaching aid. It is no substitute for relaxation teaching but may on occasion augment it.

The user puts the electrodes on his fingertips and adjusts the knob to produce a continuous tone (some instruments use a visual signal instead). Excitement, anger and any arousal causes changes in the sweat glands preparatory to sweating and causes the pitch of the sound to rise. Conversely, relaxation raises the resistance of the skin to electricity and lowers the pitch.

In this way the user can hear how the body reacts to fear when there is a sudden noise such as a loud clap or the ringing of the telephone and also to changes in his thoughts. The pitch rises in the same way when he feels

This working chair gives good back support and is high enough to allow shoulders to stay relaxed. It is also the right height for typing.

enthusiastic, angry or fearful. As Hans Selye has shown, the body responds in the same way whether the stress is pleasant or unpleasant, and with biofeedback the user can hear it doing so.

As soon as the subject relaxes the pitch drops, and as he becomes quieter and more at ease the tone will change to a low growl. After a few moments of peace the instrument ticks gently and eventually the sound dies away completely. We have found that after a few sessions the user manages without this aid, using the instrument only for occasions when a boost to assessing relaxation is required.

Although I have found biofeedback machines useful, many people dislike their mechanical nature and prefer a more natural method such as the methods of testing relaxation given above.

Posture and muscle tension

It is the back that suffers most from the abuses caused by our way of living. The bones, muscles, ligaments and discs that make up the structure of the back have a considerable strain to bear. To counteract the strain, the spine has

Posture reflects emotion

The droop of fatigue and dejection

Over-alert posture with hollow back

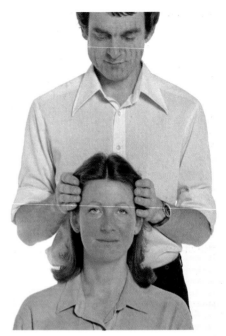

Holding your head habitually on one side will lead to neck and shoulder pain.

Get your partner to balance your head and remind you when you forget.

Stiff and uptight

adopted an 'S' shape with two forward curves, one in the neck and one in the lower back. In this position the spine is enabled to withstand the stresses and strains of daily living.

What is 'good' posture?

People speak of 'good' or 'bad' posture as if there were one universal posture which should be used by everyone at all times. *Any* position, good or bad, if it is held long enough, will cause the muscles to become hyper-tense, give discomfort, and, if it has become a habit, the muscles cannot readily be relaxed. The old-fashioned word 'carriage' gives a much better idea of poise

in action, of economy and grace in movement, and adaptation to continual change.

Posture frequently reflects emotional states. We are accustomed to recognize the droop of dejection, the eager alertness, the stiff uprightness of the military posture.

Individuals experiencing temporary fear, joy, aggression or grief will convey messages to other people by their posture. Sometimes these postures are transferred to others: in a research project to assess the posture of schoolchildren, it was found that where the school principal was dominating, aggressive and feared by the children, the majority of them had round backs as did many of the teachers. Where the school principal was brisk and alert and the atmosphere was of eager activity, many of the children had hollow backs.

When these emotion-expressing postures become habitual not only do they convey wrong messages to those around but some muscles will continually be working in a limited range, becoming shorter and stronger and the opposing group weaker and longer. This will eventually lead to pain and malfunction and sometimes to structural changes that cannot be remedied. The unbalanced pull may have ill effects on the spine.

Even an activity as simple as washing up can give incapacitating pain if the stooping is prolonged, so break off your work before you get really tired and have a stretch or do some exercise.

Some racquet-games players have one shoulder always held higher than the other as a result of continual practice. If they are right handed it will be the left shoulder that is high. If this position is continued for years, even when they are not playing, it can lead to a sideways curve of the spine and pain later in life. Awareness of the possibility will enable the player to

If you play racquet games be aware that ... one shoulder may become higher than the other.

Even washing up can create back strain, so break off and stretch or do some exercises.

counteract this unbalanced muscle tension, though at first it is likely that it will have to feel 'wrong' to be 'right'. Swimmers and athletic runners rarely have this unevenness of shoulders, but it is often seen amongst housewives who always carry heavy shopping bags in the same hand.

Sitting and muscle strain
If you have to spend much of your working life sitting down it is essential to choose your chair wisely. It must be one that is specifically right for you, so make a fuss about it. It should give good but not exaggerated support for the lower curve of your back, your feet should easily reach the floor, the seat edge should not press on the soft structures at the back of your knee and the height should be such that you do not have to stoop or hunch your shoulders as you work. Dr Alan Stoddard's book, *The Back-Relief from Pain*, gives some good suggestions for taking care of your back.

Playing golf
LEFT A well balanced combination of muscle relaxation and contraction.

A rocking chair is relaxing, as well as being good for your back.

Activity is important to relieve muscle tension, so break off from your work at intervals and do some of the neck and shoulder exercises shown later in the book. Some of these you can do almost unnoticed.

Head and neck posture

An exaggerated curve in the neck with a jutting forward thrust of the head will give rise to pain and some more far-reaching disability. If you sit slumped, with your back stooping, you have to make a forward curve in your neck to look forwards.

If you sit tall, with your chest lifted out of your abdomen, your eyes look straight ahead and you are unlikely to have an exaggerated curve. Good carriage of the head is important as it affects general posture. I was fortunate to have been taught by Matthias Alexander when I was at college and recall his insistence of the feeling of 'forward and up' and his skilful manipulating of ill-used spines to restore them to comfort and efficiency. His work is now carried on by Dr Wilfred Barlow whose book, *The Alexander Principle*, shows the importance of good use of muscle in maintaining good neck posture.

Check up on your head posture

Your head weighs between 12−14 lb (5−6 kg). Normally it is continually moving with the neck muscles contracting and relaxing. But if it is always held to one side the muscles which support this heavy weight will prudently ache to give you a warning which you might ignore. Some people attending a migraine relaxation class were surprised when I was able to locate an exact spot where there was pain, either just above the shoulder blade or in the neck. I knew just where I would find this because they were holding their head on one side and the muscles on the other side were overworked. They had no idea of this particular head posture; it probably originated in childhood when it was an endearing or deprecating gesture and it became stuck as a habit. No one had told them (see page 35).

Look in the mirror to check whether you hold your head easily balanced on top of your spine, neither bent to one side nor jutting forward. Get your partner to hold your head and move it gently with no opposition from you and then let it rest in a good position in the middle. If you have usually held your head to one side you will need constant reminders to help you break this habit. The head and neck movements shown later will help relieve the aches and tension.

In driving see that your back is adequately supported and hold your head well.

Note that massage is a good way of relieving the effects of muscle tension.

To sum up:

Activity helps relaxation. Move when you can.

Good carriage will minimize fatigue and muscle tension. Think tall.

Choose your chair carefully.

Get a partner to help you recognize faulty posture.

3 BEGINNING TO RELAX

Whenever you learn a new skill, whether it is swimming, playing a musical instrument, crochet or golf there are some essentials if you are to be successful. First, there must be motivation: you must have a real desire to learn. Then there must be some understanding of the basic principles involved and some idea of what you can achieve. Then there will have to be frequent practice, learning from your mistakes and successes.

It is like this with relaxation. First there must be a positive desire to take some personal responsibility for your mental and physical health without depending unnecessarily on drugs or other people. You will need some knowledge about how and why relaxation works so that learning comes with understanding. This is especially the case if you are sceptical about relaxation (as many people are at first), and you should have some idea of what you can reasonably expect to achieve. Then there will have to be disciplined, regular practice, going step by step until, like swimming or cycling, it becomes part of you and you don't have to think about it. You will find, I am sure, that the practice stages can be very enjoyable.

As you learn, remind yourself of what relaxation can do for you. Plenty of research evidence exists to back this up. It is not just my opinion or folklore conjecture. Relaxation can counteract the effects of high levels of arousal and the stress disorders these generate, it can dispel the fatigue and aches that are caused by prolonged muscle tension, it can help you tolerate pain, make personal relationships easier and give feelings of well being and aid restorative sleep.

There are, of course, some things relaxation cannot do. It is no cure for conditions that require medical or surgical treatment, though it may well help them, and will be of great benefit in the recovery period. Relaxation cannot remove personal or work problems but you can learn to diminish your reaction to them and this in itself may go part of the way towards solving them. When you are more relaxed, it is easier to talk over your problems with someone else.

When and how to practise

Make time for learning and practice. You are never too busy to relax for some time in the day. If you say you are, it is because you don't really want to. Churchill always took time off to relax, even while prime minister during the Second World War. Thomas Edison relaxed often during the day so that he could diminish the amount of time he spent sleeping at night. I know several businessmen who practise relaxation every day in the office after lunch and this period is honoured by their staff; a group of typists relax together in the lunch hour and give each other shoulder massage to relieve muscle tension. I know a group of nuns in a teaching order who have a relaxation class before prayer and meditation; housewives who have a ten-minute break in mid-morning when the chores are finished; busy salesmen simmer down and relax in the car inbetween visits. All these busy people find time to relax and discover it improves their efficiency.

Remember that you do not have to lie down to relax. You can practise in a bus, in an office chair, under a hair dryer, in fact, in most situations, however crowded or chaotic they may be.

Some businessmen are afraid to relax, thinking that if they do they may risk losing their efficiency and drive. The opposite is the case for, by conserving energy for the things that really matter, they can achieve more with less cost to their health. Others feel guilty at letting go and believe they must use every unforgiving minute of each day, even though some of the activity is fruitless. They would serve other people better if they would take some time off to replenish their resources, even if this occasionally means letting people down. Most households simmer down when the mother is relaxed and this is far more important than an immaculate home. There is more to home-making than house-keeping and more to parenthood than hygiene. A simple meal eaten in a happy atmosphere is more enjoyable, and better digested, than a gourmet dinner served by an exhausted cook seething with resentment.

When you practise, go slowly. Relaxation is ease. It is 'not doing' rather than 'doing' and there will be some unlearning. Your tension may have become a life-time habit and the addiction will not be easy to relinquish. So don't expect results immediately though you should feel some benefits after a few weeks.

Get a partner to work with you if you can. It is more fun this way and laughter itself releases tension. Your partner can help you to recognize muscle tension and relaxation, give reminders during the day and help with soothing massage. If it is your spouse who triggers off tension, he or she may not be the best helper at first but other couples will enjoy working together. Best of all is to learn with a group of people who all help each other. It is quite possible to learn on your own, however, and sometimes a relaxation record or cassette gives additional help.

Plan for adequate sleep but don't go to sleep when you are practising. I have heard people say that they have no need to relax because they can drop off to sleep anywhere. But they are often the people who either use sleep as a way of escaping from problems or who are so keyed up when they sleep that they grind their teeth at night, gripping their fists so tightly that there may be fingermarks on their palms in the morning. It is no wonder they feel exhausted after a night's sleep. So save your sleeping for when you have finished practice.

Don't believe that because your mind is agitated relaxation won't help. Those who say that it is their mind that needs relaxing and not their body should understand that emotions and thinking are always accompanied by some muscle tension and that the opposite, muscle relaxation, will help the agitation to quieten down. It is of course much more difficult to learn when you are in a state of great anxiety and that is why I urge people to learn it as a preventative measure; children should be taught relaxation as part of their physical education. Even in a state of great anxiety, however, the physical release of the exercises will help.

Why physical relaxation first?

We have all known high-powered men and women who cannot let up for a moment. They take on more and more responsibilities even though those around can see that, unless their way of life is changed, there will be inevitable damage to health and happiness.

It is a massive task to alter your way of life, and attitudes are hard to change. No amount of lecturing will help. Relaxation learnt as a physical skill is easier and the learning presents something of a challenge. Once you have discovered how pleasant it is to feel relaxed, when you learn that you do not need the continual 'high' of adrenalin, and other stress hormones, you will begin to adapt your way of life so that it is not so stressful.

This was brought home to me by a man who was director of six companies and was facing the threat of severe breakdown in health. He came to a series of relaxation classes and after several sessions he suddenly became aware of the frenetic aspect of his business life: the frequent trips across the world, the working at all hours of the day and night, his inability to face leisure, the disruption of his family life. He had been admonished by his physician, his family and colleagues but to no avail. He said that relaxation had given him greater self-knowledge and for the first time he could accept the idea and the pleasure of letting go for a while. He took stock of his life, assessed the priorities and gave up some of the less important activities. In a characteristic way he practised relaxation seriously and both his health and work improved.

So learn how to relax the muscles of the body first, then, when you can do this a little, go on to deep relaxation. After this, if you feel you need more help you can go on to other mind-stilling techniques such as meditation, but not everyone will need this. Those who do will find that relaxation enhances these other experiences.

4 BREATHING AND RELAXATION

Most systems of relaxation include methods of controlled breathing. Some of these are complicated or strange while others are unnecessarily difficult. Some involve the kind of over-breathing which can result in the blood becoming too alkaline with unpleasant side-effects.

Some people habitually over-breathe and this pattern may have originated long ago. When any individual is upset, frightened or angry, changes in respiration take place and these do not follow any set pattern. There may be gasps, catching of the breath, panting or laboured breathing, a reaction which was suitable for the original occasion but which may have become an unconscious habit. When this is usual it may produce symptoms such as dizziness, faintness, numbness in the fingers, intolerance of bright lights, migraine-type headaches, excessive sighing and yawning, muscular cramps, palpitations, angina-like symptoms, flatulence and belching, anxiety, 'unreal' feelings, panic attacks, weakness, exhaustion and emotional sweating.

Dr Lum of Cambridge, England, has been involved in research into the effects and treatment of what is technically called hyper-ventilation and he suggests that the incidence of ill effects of over-breathing has been underestimated. This comes as a surprise to those of us who were brought up believing that deep breathing before an open window in mid-winter was the cure of all ills!

The kind of breathing associated with anxiety is mainly in the upper chest. You can observe this in the way the collar or neckline moves up and down markedly at each breath and the rate of breathing is fast. In contrast, slow breathing, using the lower part of the lungs with the emphasis on the outbreath, is a help in general relaxation and in relieving the symptoms of over-breathing. It often helps to understand a little about the reasons for this.

Every organ in the body requires oxygen to live, and the body needs this constant supply of oxygen as well as a means of removing waste carbon dioxide. This is the task of the blood circulation and of the lungs where the exchange of gases takes place.

The chief factor in regulating the rate and depth of breathing is not the lack of oxygen, as might have been expected, but the concentration of carbon dioxide in the blood which causes it to become more acid. It is this that makes the respiratory centre in the brain respond, and it does this very quickly. By over-breathing, however (taking in more air than the body needs), too much carbon dioxide is 'washed' out of the blood and various disorders may occur.

People who have anxieties about breathing are usually very concerned to make sure that there are open windows, and may find public meetings cause them distress if windows are closed and they feel they must gasp for air. It is not the oxygen they need but the carbon dioxide they have been breathing out excessively. If this is your problem, relaxation will help to diminish your anxiety, and calm, slow

As you breathe in, your hands rise and separate a little.

breathing with the emphasis on the outbreath will relieve the odd symptoms. There is no need to concentrate on breathing in, the body takes care of that and will take all it needs. Concentrate on breathing out when you practise, then forget about it.

Breathing, muscle tension and relaxation

There is a useful link between breathing and relaxation. Try this: tighten up all your muscles as hard as you can ... very tight ... then tighter. Then let go and relax. You probably found that, as you tightened up, you held your breath and as you relaxed you let it go. This link between the outbreath and relaxation is a useful one and can be used whenever you practise (there will be no need again to tighten up first).

You may also have noticed that your abdominal muscles contracted in the way they do whenever you are anxious or alert. This exercise therefore combines calm breathing with relaxation of abdominal muscles.

Put one hand on the upper part of your chest and the other on top of your abdomen (on top of the bulge if you have one). Exhale first, then inhale comfortably. If you are doing this correctly your abdomen rises at the start of the breath, but if your chest moved first this is an inefficient kind of breathing.

Do it again several times and try to breathe so that there is very little movement in the upper chest but plenty under your lower hand. Later on you will find that your back is also involved in breathing and your lower ribs spread sideways. Don't bother much about this. Every time you breathe out do it *slowly* with a slight

45

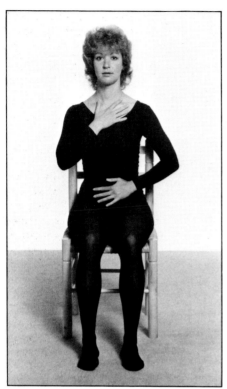

Check up on your breathing. The lower hand should rise first and the top one hardly at all.

Improving lung capacity

Although there are many advocates of deep breathing exercises to improve the capacity of the lungs, probably the better way is by taking regular and sensible physical activity requiring some muscular effort. In this way the intake of oxygen is related to bodily needs and there is no need for conscious breath control. The brain takes care of that naturally as heart and lungs respond to increasing demands without the need for special exercises. Breathing to help relaxation though is another matter.

Controlled breathing in everyday situations

Use calm controlled breathing whenever you have to face a difficult situation. For example, when you have an interview for a job or with an awkward boss, breathe calmly and slowly two or three times before the interview begins. Public speaking can be alarming for those not used to it but even experienced speakers use breathing techniques to help them calm down before they begin. Most singers and actors will have learnt diaphragmatic breathing as part of their training. Use calm breathing to simmer down after a row (if there isn't the opportunity to get rid of the feelings by physical activity). If you have to receive an injection, a slow outbreath coupled with relaxation as the needle goes in can remove the apprehension and discomfort.

sigh, rather like a balloon gently deflating. After exhaling, pause a moment and let the breath come in just as much as the body wants; don't exaggerate the breathing in, let it happen. Combine the outbreath with relaxation whenever you practise. Two or three of these calm breaths are enough at the beginning of relaxation practice. In deep relaxation you will find that the body requires less oxygen and less carbon dioxide is produced so the breathing becomes shallow, slow and gentle.

You may find it easier to practise lying down. Let your hands rise as you breathe in.

If you are the sort of person who weeps easily on occasions when it would be inappropriate to do so (a good cry is often a great help to release tension but there are many occasions when it would be embarrassing to do so) try taking a deep breath and hold it while you bear down hard. This pushes the sob down until you can control it. Then breathe calmly and evenly again. Note that this controlled breathing is only used as an aid to relaxation, it has no relation to the body's needs for air. But it does help to calm the flutterings and reduces the rate of panic breathing and the unpleasant feelings it brings.

For those who are anxious about their breathing

A few people, especially those who have been anxious for a long time, find that any attention to breathing is disturbing and increases the anxiety. If you feel like this, skip this section for a while and come back to it later when you have learnt to relax. Whenever you get tense about your breathing, don't gulp for more and more air but breathe *out* slowly as far as you can and then let the air come into your lungs without effort.

Breathing, yoga and meditation

Breath control has been used as part of the meditative routines of most of the oriental religions for several thousand years. Zen Buddhist meditation ('Zen' means meditation) involves close attention to breathing for long periods; this aids the exclusion of distracting thoughts in the search for enlightenment.

Most yoga systems include breath control and some of the advanced techniques are complicated and strange to western ideas. Some may be inappropriate and unwise for those unused to the methods of the east where the teaching is done individually and over very long periods. For the purposes of relaxation in everyday situations complicated breathing systems are unsuitable.

Hatha yoga, however, easily adapts to western ideas. It is concerned with physical health and involves the practice of various postures accompanied by controlled breathing and relaxation. The postures undoubtedly increase flexibility and bodily control, and in acquiring them while breathing in a special way the concentration required often brings about mental relaxation. Be careful though about some of the postures because, although teachers are always very careful to insist that there should be no strain, man is a competitive being and finds it difficult not to attempt as much as others and if possible to surpass them. So take care over postures that involve extreme flexion of the back and neck and don't be tempted to over-breathe. There are many men, women and children who testify to the benefits obtained form this gently absorbing form of body control. Learning to recognize relaxation will add to the value of yoga sessions.

5 RELAXATION EXERCISES

Give all the exercises a good try first then select the ones that suit you. People differ in what helps them to understand muscle relaxation; for example, I had a man in my classes who had been in the army for many years. He was quite unable to relax in any of the standing exercises, it was against all his training. Once he was lying on the floor, however, he was able to relax his arms and the understanding grew from then on. In contrast, one housewife who had tried several other methods of relaxation, found her greatest help came from the arm-swinging exercises; she even re-arranged her kitchen so that she had room for practice, and only later could she relax fully in the lying position. So find out what helps you most and then stick to your own routine while you are learning.

For convenience I have arranged the exercises so that the standing ones come first, then sitting, then lying down. I will mention when a partner can assist and when massage will be helpful. Full deep relaxation comes only after you have learnt to relax the various parts of the body (you don't have to be expert at this, just a little reduction in tension helps).

Have a really good stretch — reach up and out, perhaps with a yawn.

Standing

Stretch   Have a good stretch before you begin to relax. Notice how a cat gives a whole-body stretch and yawn before it settles down.

Stretch up and out as far as you can. If you feel like it, yawn.

Stretch up with one arm, let it drop and relax, then stretch both arms together.

Up with one arm as far as you can go, then let it relax and drop. Do the same with the other arm.

Then reach with both arms before letting them drop and relax at your sides.

Floppy jog Let your arms go floppy and do a relaxed jog on the spot. Your feet hardly leave the ground. This, and many other exercises are more fun done to music.

Arms

Floppy sway Stand with your feet astride to give you a good base. Lean a little way forward (not far, mind your back). Let your arms dangle straight down. Sway a little so that your arms move as a result. Then let them gradually come to a standstill. Get a partner to test how relaxed they are. He should lift one arm just above the elbow joint and it should feel heavy. When he lets go the arm drops immediately and you neither help nor hinder.

You can learn a lot about differences in relaxing if you test a number of people this way.

Floppy sway Let your arms dangle . . .

Swimmers' shake (Swimmers often do this to loosen up before races.) Shake one arm with a rotatory movement from your wrist up to your shoulder so that the arm muscles wobble. This is only successful if your arm hangs straight down, so don't lift it sideways. You can add to this a relaxed shake of your whole body.

The swish Raise your arms in front at shoulder height. Let them flop loosely so that they swish past your thighs. Do this with relaxed arms for as long as you like, registering the feel of loose arms, and then end the sequence with a complete circle of your arms backwards. This helps to keep your shoulder joints mobile.

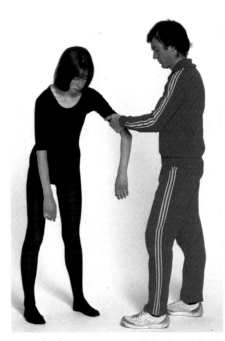

. . . and when one arm is picked up it feels heavy.

The swish

Circling shoulders

Raise your arms to shoulder height.

Circle one shoulder backwards . . .

Let your arms drop loosely to swish past your sides. Repeat rhythmically.

. . . then the other, to release shoulder tension. Then circle both shoulders backwards at the same time.

Big circle
Warm up with the big circle.

Bend your knees and
reach out to the side.

Begin to make a big
circle with your hand.

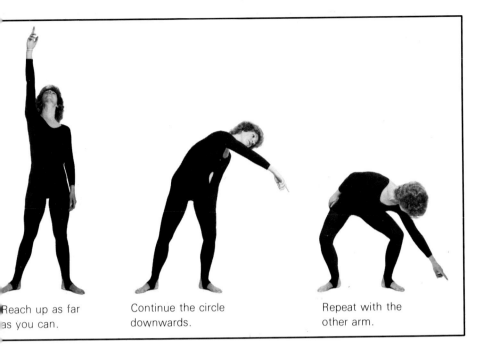

Reach up as far as you can.

Continue the circle downwards.

Repeat with the other arm.

Warming-up exercises

Athletes always do some exercises to warm up before strenuous activity to avoid the risk of injury when muscles are tense. Warm muscles relax more easily.

Slapping Slap the muscles all over your body. There is an added advantage in this as it tones up the muscles, so pay especial attention to the thighs and abdomen.

Big circle Large trunk movements provide the most effective way of warming up. Warning! Don't let anyone persuade you to touch your toes with your legs straight unless you are very supple and fit. It has little value and can hurt your back. So bend your knees as you reach down in the big circle.

Reach to the side and with your finger draw the largest circle in the air you possibly can, making big trunk movements in stretching, bending and turning. If you are short of space you can do this with your elbow making the circle instead of your hand.

Warm up and tone your muscles by slapping yourself with relaxed hands.

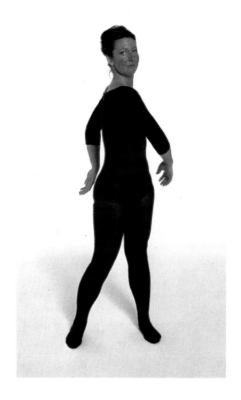

The chairoplane This isn't easy at first but once you have got it going it does give a good feeling of relaxation.

Lead up to the exercise this way. Stand with your feet apart with your arms loosely by your sides. Twist your trunk so that your hips and shoulders face one way. Your arms are still by your sides. Turn to the other side. Then make this a rhythmical movement, turning from side to side and as you do this your arms float up of their own accord. Speed this up a little and your arms will float up and even wrap round you if they are relaxed. If you feel giddy, either close your eyes or, better still, keep your head facing forward as you turn. This exercise feels good when you have got it right: it just happens.

Sitting

Shoulders

Many people show tension in their shoulders and it is of two kinds: some hunch them and others draw them down stiffly. Sometimes these muscles remain contracted all day and as a result they become aching and tender to touch. Women who always carry shopping bags in one hand may find this an additional strain.

Hunch and pull Tighten your shoulders just a *little*. This is only the amount of tension you use when you are fussed and anxious. Recognize this and let the tension go so that your shoulders drop. Then relax them even further.

The chairoplane – you can feel your arms relax as they float round while you turn.

A partner can feel the effects of slight tension this way: hands rest on top of the shoulders and when you tighten up even slightly he can feel the muscles tense. It is easy to understand why they ache when they are always held like this.

Then pull your shoulders down, keeping your neck long. Recognize this form of stiffness and then relax the muscles.

Circling shoulders Circle your shoulders to relieve muscle tension and improve circulation. You can do this almost unobserved whenever your shoulders ache, (see page 51).

Massage by a partner is a great help in relieving muscle tension in shoulders.

During the day, notice when you hold these muscles tight: it may be when you are driving, doing housework, telephoning or even when you are resting. Remember that you look more at ease and move with more grace when your shoulders are relaxed.

Flight

Stand with feet apart
and arms raised
obliquely sideways.

Drop arms loosely so
that they cross in front.

Flight

Stand with your feet astride with your arms raised obliquely sideways and upwards. Wait for a moment to feel poised and at ease, with your neck long and your shoulders relaxed. Let your arms drop downwards in a relaxed heavy way so that they cross in front of you (keep your body quite upright). Then raise your arms sideways and upwards again with a feeling of lift in your whole body so that your hands touch lightly overhead. Then let your arms fall sideways again to cross in front. Repeat this several times keeping this rhythm: 'Drop, and lift, and touch . . . drop, lift, and touch'. You may prefer to lift the arms just obliquely upwards instead of the whole way in which case it will be 'Drop and lift, drop and lift'. Whichever way you do it you will capture the delightful feeling of relaxed loose arms and the poised feeling of flight.

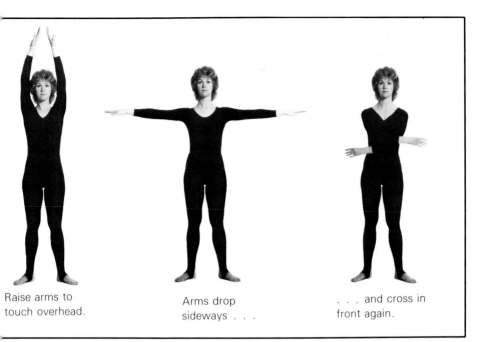

Raise arms to
touch overhead.

Arms drop
sideways . . .

. . . and cross in
front again.

Legs

Many women hold their legs tightly together even when they are alone and resting, and these large muscles need to relax sometimes. Businessmen in high-powered jobs often hold their legs tightly in committee meetings and bend an ankle strongly upwards when they are annoyed. When you are sitting at rest, let your thighs fall apart a little and keep ankles relaxed.

Hands

Notice how often people show their tension in their hands. They are probably the easiest part of the body to learn to relax and when they are it induces general relaxation.

Shake your hands loosely as if you were flicking water from your fingers.

Clench and stretch Clench your fists, then stretch out your fingers as far as they will go.

Cradle Rest with one hand cradled in the other It is impossible to grip your hands tightly when they are cradled in this way, so use this position when you relax sitting down. The message received by your brain is that you are quiet and at rest so there is no need to be on guard. Use it also when you are feeling tense, for example, at the dentist, at take-off in a plane, watching television, waiting in the surgery. I know a busy physician who deliberately relaxes his hands while he is waiting for his next patient; he also notices signs of tension in his patients' hands. If you are doing intricate manual work, or typing, break off when you are tired and do a few hand exercises. Relaxed hands and arms are necessary for musicians and you will notice that eminent performers have beautiful relaxation in their movements.

57

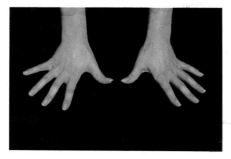

Stretch your hands as wide as they will go.

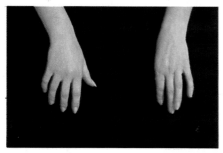

Then rest them loosely.

Or: Cradle one hand in the other when relaxing sitting down.

Face

There is a very close relationship between the state of the muscles of the face and a state of mind. Much of our communication with other people is non-verbal, and a tense anxious face signals to everyone messages of anxiety, and this is very catching. A forehead in a state of continual contraction also contributes to tension headaches.

First check up to make sure that your teeth are not held tightly together. The only time they need to meet is when you are eating, so let the jaw rest in the relaxed position.

Do the following exercise once only. There will be no need to do it again but it helps if you can observe the effects of emotions on forehead muscles, and realize the kind of message it gives to others.

Do this facing a mirror, or, if you can bear it, facing someone else:

Frown This represents the fight reaction.

Raise your eyebrows This represents surprise or flight.

Do both of these together This represents conflict, when you can neither fight nor run away and it conveys a message of anguish and anxiety.

Now relax the muscles so that your forehead feels wider and higher than it

If forehead muscles remain tense it may lead to headaches and strain. The frown *left* shows fight and the raised eyebrows *right*, flight.

Turn your head slowly and evenly from one side to the other. Keep your head upright.

Let your head bend to one side . . .

. . . then the other. Remember to keep your shoulders level.

did before. Give your forehead some massage to smooth out the worry muscles or better still get someone else to do it for you.

Palming After a spell of concentrated mental work, 'palming' gives relief for eyes and neck.

Lean forward and rest your forehead on your cupped hands, hands crossed over your eyes, with your eyes closed. Combine this with relaxation and controlled breathing.

Neck

Make sure that your head is held in the middle and not to one side, or jutting forward. You can see this in a mirror, or get a partner to help you. He should stand behind you holding your head with his hands, and move it very gently with no opposition from you and then place it in the correct position. It may feel wrong to you but keep it there (see page 51).

Turn your head to look first one way and then the other, keeping your shoulders square all the time.

Bend your head from side to side keeping your shoulders level.

Drop your head forward then lift it so that your head is held high. Keep your shoulders down and reach up with the back part of your head as if you were being pulled up by a tuft of hair at the back.

Some people, especially older ones, may get giddy if the head is bent far backwards so I do not include this. A small head roll, however, is useful to release tension in the neck.

Massage for the back of the neck is very helpful in releasing neck tension.

Neck press Sit with your neck well supported by a high-backed chair, or put a kitchen-type chair against the wall (use a cushion for your head if you like).

Press your neck hard against the support so that as much of it touches as possible. Then release the tension and let the muscles relax.

A neck-support pillow is useful for those whose neck is particularly curved forward or if there is neck pain.

Lips and cheeks Pursed lips and tight cheeks may signal a wrong message to those around and make you look disapproving and severe. Photographic models often massage their lips to make them look relaxed.

Massaging lips softens up the whole of the lower face.

Good musicians know how relaxation improves performance.

These exercises relieve tension and pain in lower back and improve posture.

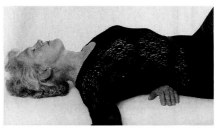

Lie on the floor with your knees bent (use a cushion under your head if you prefer) Make a SLIGHT hollow back and place your hand under it.

Then squeeze your hand against the ground, take your hand away and go on pressing. Your pelvis will have tilted and your abdominal muscles contracted. Do this several times. Later on there will be no need to place your hand underneath.

Neck

Press your neck hard against the floor and then release the tension. Your partner can test neck relaxation as shown on page 31.

Abdominal and back muscles

This is probably more comfortable if you lie with knees bent. Press your back hard into the ground so that every part is touching. At the same time, draw in your tummy muscles (don't hold your breath). Then enjoy the relief of relaxation of back and tummy muscles. Abdominal breathing also helps the abdominal muscles to relax. Some people react to stress by contracting abdominal muscles as if they were continually expecting a blow. This can make these muscles ache and add to fatigue and discomfort, so try to recognize this and let them relax.

Eyes

Close your eyes softly and relax all your muscles. Imagine you are looking at something in the distance. Visualize it as vividly as you can. Then visualize something very close to you for a few seconds. Then relax the eye muscles so that they rest in-between.

If your eyes flicker a lot when you are practising deep relaxation, don't bother about it. Just think about relaxing other parts of the body and eventually you will find that the eye flickering has stopped. It is better not to do anything directly about it.

Do this pelvic correction exercise when you are standing. Bend your knees slightly so that you avoid bracing them, and stand tall. Place one hand below your tummy and the other flat at the base of your spine with your fingers facing downwards. Tilt your pelvis so that your tail is tucked under and the front of the pelvis raised. Take your hands away and register this position. Do this several times without the aid of your hands.

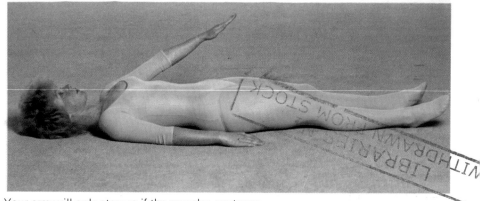

Your arm will only stay up if the muscles are tense.

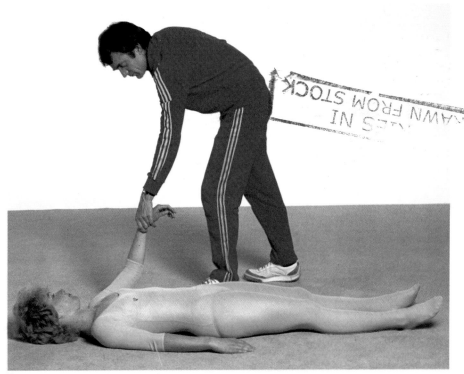

Partner tests relaxation: arms feels floppy and heavy.

SCIENCE

Squeeze your legs together, bend ankles up, and press legs down hard.

Beginning to relax – let your legs fall open . . .

. . . until legs, ankles and toes are fully relaxed.

These exercises below will loosen tight shoulders and expand the chest.

Sit or stand tall and place your fingertips on top of your shoulders. Circle your elbows backwards.

Sit on a chair and reach up. Clasp your hands behind you and raise them as you lift your chest. This can often relieve high backache.

Some tips for coping with job stress

1. List tasks in order of priority:
   a. things that must be done;
   b. things that ought to be done;
   c. things that can wait.
   Then ruthlessly discard c., delegate as much of b. as you can, and get to work at once on a.

2. If you work in an office, keep your desk clear.

3. Don't procrastinate. Recognize all the tricks you use to put off getting down to work.

4. When demands are too great, have the courage to say *no*.

5. Work off your stress with vigorous exercise. Run up and down stairs, do some exercises, go for a run (but don't become a fanatic).

6. Communicate. Let others know how you feel. Discuss your problem with someone you trust.

7. Acknowledge the effort or success of others at work or at home. One of the major sources of stress is lack of appreciation. If you give this to others they will work better, and maybe they will also appreciate you.

8. Keep fit. This will involve good nutrition, sensible exercise and adequate sleep.

9. Use a stress reduction technique. This could be muscle relaxation (a cassette is helpful), meditation, biofeedback or other methods. If this is impossible at work, have some 'time-out' relaxation in a parked car at lunch time or before you travel home. This really helps you to be more efficient.

10. Recognize when you are reaching fatigue point and take action to remedy this.

11. Make time for family and friends.

12. Have an absorbing hobby.

13. Practise coping. Recognize your particular source of stress and while you are fully relaxed, visualize a typical stressful situation. See yourself coping in a calm and masterful way. This is a useful way of preparing yourself to cope.

14. Travel stress. If driving to work in the rush hour makes you irritable and tired, use traffic jams to practise relaxing shoulders and face and to breathe calmly. You will arrive at work less tired and with more energy. Otherwise use alternative transport.

15. In a crisis, use the emergency STOP technique (see page 66).

16. Remember the holistic approach to health: a balance between physical, mental and spiritual life.

Stop!

An emergency quick relaxation technique

There are some stressful occasions that call for a quick relaxation technique to stop a rapid build-up of tension, especially when there is no opportunity of relieving it by physical activity. A shop assistant may feel enraged by the behaviour of a difficult and rude customer but cannot lash out as she would like; a harrassed housewife may be overwhelmed by feelings of fear as she prepares for a dinner party; a worker may be humiliated by his boss but cannot fight or run away. Some people have sudden feelings of panic in the street or in a lift and need a quick relaxation technique to cope; a car driver may feel frustrated and dangerously angry at someone else's bad driving, or find himself trembling with anxiety over delays before an appointment. A simple emergency technique will help to lower the tension.

Remember that mental stress will lessen when you relax muscles. This really does happen, even when you may be in a situation where only partial relaxation is possible. Don't believe that you are the sort of person who can never relax. You can. Everyone can to some degree, but strong feelings of tension make relaxation difficult especially if they are allowed to build up. So recognize your feelings of tension (even if these seem to you to be weird and alarming). Accept them for what they are. Use the STOP! technique to lower the arousal and bring it back to manageable limits. Do this before it gets out of hand.

Say sharply to yourself, aloud if the situation permits, 'STOP!' This means stop fussing, stop getting so worked up. Then breathe in and hold your breath for a moment (generally you should *not* pause between inhaling and exhaling, but in this sort of emergency it may help. But don't hold it for more than a moment.) Then breathe out *slowly* and, as you do, relax your shoulders and hands. Pause for a moment then breathe in again. As you breathe out slowly this time, relax your forehead and jaw. Stay quiet for a few seconds then go on with whatever you were doing, but move smoothly and slowly. If you have to talk, speak a little more slowly and with your voice a little lower than usual.

This STOP! relaxation can usually be done without anyone noticing and you will find that, in spite of your feelings, the tension will lessen.

6 DEEP RELAXATION

So far the exercises have been concerned with localized muscle relaxation, learning to recognize tension, releasing it when you wish and applying it to daily living situations. The deepest experience of relaxation, however, comes when all voluntary muscles are relaxed with the body fully supported and the mind shut off from its problems. When this state is achieved there is an indescribable sense of peace and tranquillity, the mind idles gently and there is full physical and mental rest. Eventually for some people there comes an experience which transcends ordinary consciousness.

It takes time and practice to attain this, so don't expect this all at once. Nor is the complete experience wholly necessary because even a short period of whole-body relaxation will be recuperative and delightful. Excessive use of deep relaxation and other similar techniques defeats its beneficial results. The aim is not to withdraw from the world and turn inwards for long periods but to maintain a balance between mental and physical activity and rest. Ten to twenty minutes once or twice a day is sufficient. If you are short of sleep you can follow the practice with a nap. On the other hand, some people drop off to sleep too easily (as I have found to my cost when I have been lecturing. The mere mention of 'relaxation' is enough to make some people doze even when the rest of the audience is all ears.). If you sleep easily it is better not to be too comfortable when you practise.

Although it is easier to relax deeply when you are lying down, it should also be practised sitting in an upright office chair or in an armchair so that you can relax in any position and in a variety of circumstances.

At first you may find it helpful to have a friend read the instructions to you, or use a tape recording or disc. You might even make a recording for yourself. You won't need this help later. If you are helping someone else, speak slowly, clearly and calmly. Your ordinary voice is best but keep the pitch low and make good pauses between instructions. There is no advantage in whispering or droning in hypnotic fashion.

The instructions below are those I use with patients and class members when I teach relaxation. They are also the ones used in the recording they use as a reminder.

Five-minute relaxation sitting in a chair

This is a simple form of relaxation for the occasions when you have only a short time to spare, say, in the office when pressures are mounting or at home when it is not possible to lie down for a longer period. If you have a chair with arm-rests you will be more comfortable, but it is possible to feel well relaxed after a short spell in an upright chair. Use a cushion in the small of your back if it helps.

You should be able to relax even in an office chair.

Try to ensure a full five minutes of undisturbed quiet.

Sit upright and well back in your chair so that your thighs and back are supported and rest your hands in the cradled position on your lap, or, if you prefer, resting lightly on top of your thighs. Let your feet rest on the ground just beneath your knees.

Instructions

Close your eyes gently. Settle down comfortably.

Begin by breathing *out* first. Then breathe in easily just as much as you need. Now breathe out *slowly* with a slight sigh, like a balloon slowly deflating. Do this once more, very slowly, and as you breathe out feel the tension begin to drain away. Then go back to your ordinary breathing, even, quiet and steady.

Now direct your thoughts to each part of your body in turn, to the muscles and joints.

Think first about your left foot. Your toes are relaxed and still. Check up on this because some people move them when they are tense. Your foot is resting easily on the floor.

Now your right foot ... toes ... ankles.

Now think about your legs. Your thighs roll *outwards* when they are relaxed so let them go.

Your back muscles will relax when you hold yourself easily upright and the spine is supported by the back of the chair.

Let your abdominal muscles become soft and relaxed. There is no need to hold your tummy in tightly. It rises and falls as you breathe quietly.

Think about the fingers of your left hand. They are curved, limp, and quite still. Now the fingers of your right hand ... relaxed, soft and still. This feeling of relaxation spreads up your arms to your shoulders.

Let your shoulders relax. Let them drop easily. Then let them relax even further than you thought they could.

Your neck muscles will relax if your head is held upright, resting easily balanced on the top of your spine, or supported against the back of the chair.

Let your face relax. Let the expression come off it.

Make sure your teeth are not held tightly together and let your jaw rest in its relaxed position.

Your cheeks are soft because there is no need to keep up an expression. Your lips are soft and hardly touching.

Relax your forehead so that it feels a little wider and a little higher than before.

Now, instead of thinking of yourself in parts, become aware of the all-over sensation of letting go, of quiet and rest.

When your muscles are relaxed, you begin to feel peaceful, and rested and quiet.

Stay like this, listening to your breathing if it helps. Sometimes after half a minute you may find your mind becoming busy and active again. If so, go through the routine again, checking up where muscles have tensed, and relaxing them. Then spend the rest of

Some alternative positions for relaxing

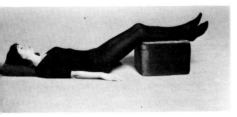

A soft stool, supporting the legs, sometimes helps blood circulation.

The plank (or strong ironing board) is at a comfortable angle.

This half-on-one-side position relaxes abdominal muscles.

A pillow under the tummy prevents back tension.

the five minutes relaxing quietly.

When the time is up, wriggle your hands and legs a little. Then open your eyes and sit quietly for a moment. When you first try it, choose a time when you are not very agitated. Later

on you can use it at any time to calm down and relax.

Have a stretch, perhaps a yawn and you will feel refreshed and alert again.

This really does help. You have to experience it several times to realize how even five minutes of deep relaxation is effective in calming you down and increasing efficiency. It requires some discipline, and the time it is most necessary is when you feel you don't need it or when you consider you are too busy to spend even five minutes gathering up your inner forces. So plan for it, and you will soon increase your skill at this quick relaxation procedure.

Deep relaxation lying down

This is for when you have at least fifteen minutes for relaxation, with an opportunity to sleep afterwards if need be. You can relax through noise and discomfort but you must be warm, so cover up well. After a spell of deep relaxation lying down, the limbs often glow with warmth, but this means that you cool down quickly and feel shivery afterwards if the room is cold. Take off your shoes and loosen tight clothing. Practise first on a firm surface, not on a bed. A carpeted floor is ideal provided it is free from draughts.

Choose the position most suitable for you

If you are young and if you have a straight back lie without a pillow, with your arms and legs a little way apart. A few people find that they feel safer if hands rest on top of the abdomen. It gives a feeling of containment to very tense people.

If you are plump, round shouldered, or are breathless or wheezy you will be better relaxing with one or two pillows under your head.

To be really comfortable, have pillows under your head and also under your knees so that the abdominal muscles relax easily.

Some people find it restful to support their legs on a low stuffed seat after they come in tired after shopping or standing for long periods. The support must be very soft so that there is no pressure on the soft structures at the back of the leg.

If you have varicose veins, piles, or slight prolapse you will find it helpful to raise your hips above your shoulders. Be careful how you get on to the plank. Don't sit suddenly in the middle or you may break it. Lie alongside it first. After a while in a raised position you can feel your internal organs settling back to their proper place. It is a very moderate version of the yoga inverted posture.

When you settle down you may begin to think of all the things you ought to be doing. But relaxation now will mean time saved in the end and your work will benefit, so will those near to you. So don't feel guilty about it, just enjoy this recuperative time out. If you are afraid of spending too long relaxing, use a kitchen timer. But you must muffle it or place it far enough away not to be startling. Some people like to play some music so softly that it doesn't have to be listened to but which will give an indication when the relaxation time is over.

By now, you will have learnt to recognize tension so there is no need to contract muscles before you relax, but a good stretch may be helpful.

Instructions for a longer spell of deep relaxation

Make yourself comfortable. Snuggle down and settle your body so that it feels limp.

Begin by letting your breath out then breathe in as far as you want. Wait for just a moment, then breathe out *slowly*, relaxing into the floor as you do so. Do this once more, very slowly and, as you breathe out, feel the tension draining away. Now go back to your ordinary breathing. Keep it even, calm, easy, then forget about it.

Think about your left foot. Your toes are quite still and your ankle is rolling outwards. Then the other foot . . . your toes . . . your ankles.

Let the feeling of relaxation spread up your legs so that they are resting heavily on the ground. The floor is doing all the supporting so there is no need for the muscles to work. Your thighs roll outwards when they are relaxed. They are sagging and heavy.

Now let the relaxation spread to the pelvic area and let all those muscles relax. Your hips rest heavily on the floor.

Feel your spine touching the floor and let the muscles of your back relax. Let your abdominal muscles go soft and loose. As you breathe evenly and calmly these muscles rise and fall.

Think about the fingers of your left hand. They are limp, still and curved. Then let that feeling of relaxation spread up your arm. It is fully supported by the floor so there is no need for the muscles to work. You can feel the contact with the floor. Now do the same with your right arm . . . your fingers still and curved, your arm floppy and loose.

Now your shoulders. Let them go. Now let them go even further.

Your neck muscles will relax when your head takes its fair share of the weight. It should be resting quite heavily on the floor or the pillow. You are not holding it at all. Let it rest.

Now your face. Make sure you are not holding your teeth tightly together. When you can let those worry muscles relax on your forehead the feeling of calm and peace spreads to the rest of the body. When you relax, your forehead feels a little wider and a little higher than before. This spreads to the scalp so that any tension there gently fades.

Your eyes are closed softly, with the eyelids still. If it helps you, relax your eye muscles this way: imagine you are looking into the distance and visualize something on the horizon. Now switch to looking at something near. Now let your eyes rest easily inbetween.

Your lips are soft and hardly touching and your tongue is shapeless. Make sure it is not pressed hard against the roof of your mouth.

Your cheeks are soft and relaxed because there is no need to keep an expression on your face.

Now, instead of thinking of yourself in parts, be aware of the whole body, relaxing quite heavily on the floor. Your whole body feels relaxed and fully supported. You are not working at all. Let all the tension go. Then a little more than you thought you could.

Stay quietly like this, and if, after half a minute, you find your mind is busy and active again, check up on each part of your body and let it relax.

When images drift into your mind, just acknowledge them and let them pass. You are acting as a bystander, interested but not involved.

Soon, as your muscles relax, you will begin to feel peaceful, and at rest . . .

At this stage, some people find it helpful to add other mind-stilling techniques, but others may find it irksome and unnecessary when they are already feeling calm and pleasantly relaxed. For those who wish to go on to meditation try one of the following suggestions:

Listen to the sound of your calm, even breathing, counting one for each in-and-out breath until you reach ten, then start again. Or . . .

visualize something that gives you pleasure, a scene, a flower, a pet Or . . .

repeat a word like 'peace', 'relax' or a short prayer. Or . . .

listen to a sound, a neutral one which has no apparent meaning.

Once you are really relaxed, your breathing becomes very gentle and slow because the body has less need of oxygen. There is a feeling of well-being as the taut muscles relax. Your arms and legs may feel almost as if they did not belong to you and there may be a sensation of floating. This may be disturbing at first but it is quite common. Later on you will either ignore it or welcome the sensation. At the end of the session, when you are feeling peaceful and relaxed, say to yourself: 'I am calm, I am relaxed.' You are not deceiving yourself, you are just registering the fact that you are relaxed.

When you have finished relaxing surface slowly. Don't get up suddenly or you may feel giddy. Move one fist, tighten it and let the tension go. Do the same with the other one. Then open your eyes and lie still and become aware of your surroundings (sometimes you may find that for a while colours appear brighter, shapes can be recognized as beautiful, there is heightened awareness). Sit up slowly, have a stretch and perhaps a yawn, and a deeper breath, then stand up. You will feel alert and refreshed and ready for work.

If you have the time and the opportunity to sleep after a session of relaxation you will find that the sleep is refreshing and untroubled. You will then be able to manage with less sleep at night.

7 MASSAGE

Massage helps muscles relax. Physiologically, massage stimulates the flow of blood and improves muscle tone. It assists in the clearing away of waste products, reduces muscular tension and its associated pain.

It does far more than this, however. During massage there is a subtle calming down of the whole body, a reduction of anxiety, and a feeling of trust develops enabling the receiver to feel rather than to think. It offers recuperative rest from the turbulance of stress.

As there are many misconceptions about the term 'massage' I must explain that I am not referring to erotic or medical massage but to an objective process which can be used by anyone who is sensitive and caring. Some of it can be done at any time, without removing clothing, though skin-to-skin contact is better. It will be understood that massage for medical conditions should only be undertaken by a qualified practitioner under medical direction.

It is only recently that we have become fully aware of the profound significance of touching for the satisfactory development of all mammals. Stroking, caressing, skin contact are almost as important to the infant as food and warmth. Touch is the first form of communication. Young animals are continually licked, nudged,

Cats love being stroked – it's all part of affectionate contact.

Fathers are parents too! The infant is reassured by close contact.

and fondled by their parents from the moment they are born and this is known to be necessary for their survival. As they get older they need to play rough-and-tumble games in close physical contact with their litter mates and parents. All young animals snuggle and cuddle against the body of the mother and it suggests a biological need for this form of reassuring contact. Experimental research with rats and puppies has shown that those who are fondled and 'gentled' in infancy show a greater increase in body weight, are more active, less fearful, have a greater ability to withstand stress and have a greater immunity to infection than those brought up in similar conditions but without the gentling experience.

This need for touching does not stop in infancy. Adult chimpanzees will pat each other, lay a hand on each other's backs in reassurance and kiss in greeting and affection. Social grooming is part of acceptance by the group. Almost all animals enjoy being stroked. Dogs seem insatiable in their appetite for fondling, cats relish being stroked and even dolphins enjoy this form of physical contact.

Humans also have this need for physical contact from birth onwards. Dr Leboyer, in his book, *Birth without Violence*, describes how babies who are gently stroked and then placed quietly in warm water, immediately after they are born, rarely scream in distress like most newborn babies but open their eyes, relax and breathe calmly. The growing child is now known to need physical contact in rough-and-tumble activities with his peers and parents, especially in pre-school years, for his satisfactory development.

Adults need physical contact too, but in many cultures, especially in the West, any touching is discouraged. The slightest accidental brushing against another requires an instant apology and people go to great lengths to avoid touching each other. It is implied that a well-bred person does not touch another except in bed. We

Contact games with father make good sense for the child's development.

pay penalties for disregarding this basic need.

Babies and young children deprived of fondling have been shown to have difficulties in their later psychological development and may have problems in making warm relationships in adulthood. But fortunately there are always second chances in life, and even with puppies it has been found that, although they may have been deprived of physical contact and gentling when they were young, they quickly catch up with the others if they have their full quota later.

For humans, massage can provide an acceptable form of fondling. It is a means of conveying friendship, sympathy and tenderness as well as serving its physiological function. When you receive massage you can indulge in the exquisite sensation of a responding skin, of letting go and being cared for. The pain and tension diminishes. Mothers have always known this when they kiss a child's hurt and rub it away to make it better.

Those who give massage gain too. There is the physical pleasure of feeling the contours of the muscles with sensitivity, the yielding of tension, the satisfaction of helping another in a unique way, and, before you realize it, there is your own relaxation also.

Massage for athletes
Some countries which are using advanced training techniques for top competitors in athletics and swimming are now turning their attention to recovery programmes. After strenuous activity the athletes are helped to recover from physical and emotional exhaustion by a programme of relaxation, baths and extensive massage. They have found that by using these methods of recovery muscular fatigue is dispelled more quickly, raised blood pressure is lowered, and massage and relaxation help to dissipate the emotional tensions caused by intense competition; future performance is enhanced without ill effects.

Self massage
Don't think that because there is no one to give you massage you must forego all the benefits. There is a lot you can do yourself to help muscles relax and relieve discomfort. Electrical massage apparatus may help but some very simple massage using your own hands is effective.

Forehead
When you feel under strain, when your eyes are tired or when a headache is imminent, smooth out the worry muscles this way:

Smooth gently from the centre outwards towards the temples.

Smooth upwards towards the hair line, one hand after the other.

Neck
When you have engaged in prolonged study or sedentary work, the muscles may prudently ache to warn you that it is time to give them a rest. The neck exercises shown on page 59 should be done first, then give your neck some massage:

Let your head rest easily, not bent forward at all so that the muscles at the back are soft. Get hold as much of the flesh as you can (it is rather like picking up a kitten by the scruff of its neck) then squeeze and let go several times.

With the tips of your fingers find the tender spots and press and let go with circular movements, without stretching the skin.

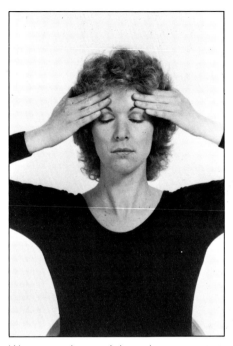

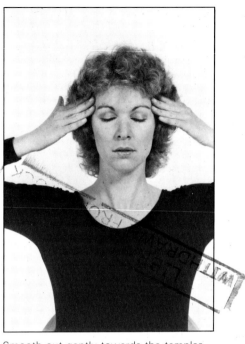

Worry muscles are tight and tense so start by smoothing sideways.

Smooth out gently towards the temples.

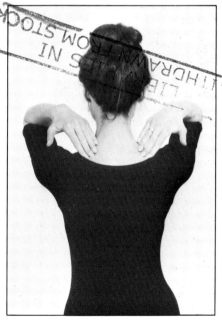

Necks can get very tight and taut. Massage helps relieve this.

Alternate squeezing, relaxing and pressing movements to stimulate blood circulation.

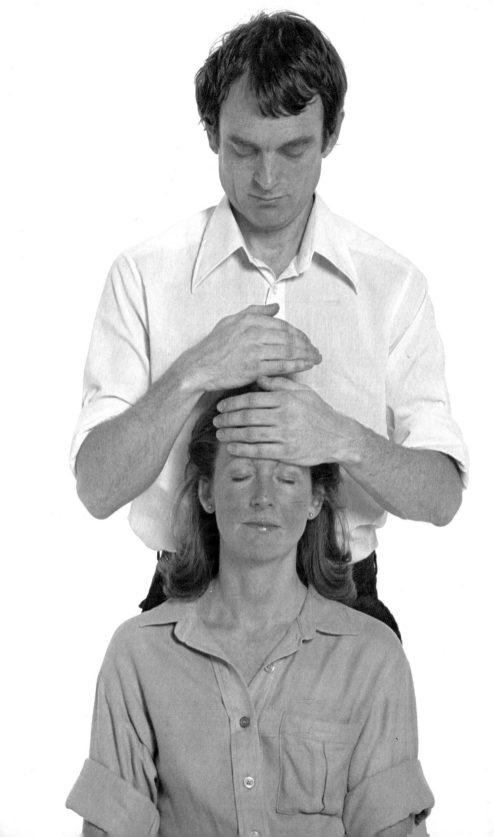

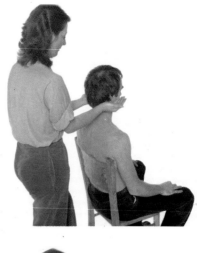

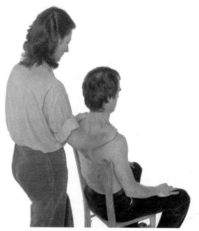

Rest your partner's head against you (*above* and *left*). Smooth gently out towards the temples, several times.

Then smooth upwards, one hand after the other, slowly and gently (*left*).

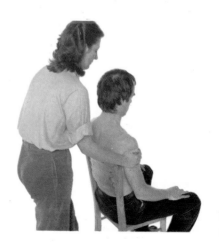

Right (read from top to bottom): Finish by gently smoothing down over neck and shoulders.

Massaging the leg muscles.

Massaging someone else

Some hints before you begin

Make sure your partner is warm because even the most relaxed muscles tighten up when they are cold. Your own hands must be warm too. If they are naturally smooth and dry there is no need to use oil or talcum powder, but if either of you is sweaty this may be helpful.

When you begin massage, place your hands on your partner and wait for a few seconds for you both to quieten down and so that you can give a message of tranquillity and confidence. It helps if you say silently to yourself: 'Relax', because then your touch conveys this to your partner.

Begin with firm purposeful movements. They become gentler later. Use the amount of pressure that suits your partner and the area of the body involved. Someone who is strongly built will prefer firm, deep massage, but a skinny bony partner will require sensitive light movements. Too much hurts, too little exasperates. Ask your partner what pressure is best but after that discourage any talking because if you ask questions your partner has to become alert to respond. You are both concerned with feeling rather than thinking.

If you are working with alternate strokes, keep one hand in contact all the time until the other takes over. Make the final stroke a decisive one and a little slower so that your partner knows it is the end. Then keep your hands motionless on the body for a moment while giving your partner time to rest or to surface gradually. Don't talk briskly until your partner is ready.

This kind of massage is not complicated if you are sensitive to your

Shoulders

Many tense people have tender spots where the muscles join on to the shoulder blade. To relieve this, try to squeeze handfuls of the muscle and let go several times, then make pressing movements with your fingertips over the tender areas (see page 75).

Legs

Give the large muscles of the thighs a shake with your hands. (You have probably seen football players and swimmers doing this to loosen up.) Then combine a kneading and squeezing movement of both hands, working alternately on each side of the thigh.

These are only a few self-massage techniques. You can adapt them for other parts of the body.

partner's feelings and will usually give an extraordinary sense of release from physical and psychological tension. There are a few people, however, who cannot bear to be touched. They are usually very tense and wary and at this stage massage is wasted on them. What should be an exquisitely delightful experience becomes a nightmare and any touching is abhorrent. In this case, don't try. They may come to it later when they are more relaxed.

Some people enjoy doing massage to music, especially if something calm and soothing is chosen. One person's pleasure in music, however, can be another's poison so it must be a joint choice. As you massage, bear in mind the two functions: the physiological one which helps circulation, the pressure on the skin emptying the blood vessels and its release allowing them to fill again; then there is the emotional function, calming down and a whole-body response of relaxation.

Remember: don't attempt to use massage for medical conditions which require expert attention, and never massage over open or very tender surfaces.

Some examples of massage for partners

These can all be done without removing clothing if it is not convenient. For example, you can help a fellow worker in the office when shoulders and neck are tense and aching or relieve a tension headache.

The basic methods for this simple massage are stroking and kneading. Stroking is of two kinds: deep stroking (called effleurage) to improve circulation and relieve muscle aches and tension, and surface stroking which is much lighter and has a calming-down effect. Effleurage is done with the flat of the hand, usually moving towards the heart, and the skin rolls in front of the hand. Surface stroking is usually done in the opposite direction, is lingering, gentle and your hands must be very relaxed. Kneading involves using the whole hand, squeezing, pressing and letting go.

To avoid fatigue, stand with a wide base with your feet apart, usually with one in front of the other. In large movements, use your whole body with transference of weight rather than pressing with fingers.

Forehead
Stand behind your partner, leaning forward a little so that her head is resting against you. If you don't do this she will have to tighten up neck muscles to keep her head still.

Check to make sure her head is held in the middle and is not bending forward or tilted to one side. Ask her to close her eyes softly. Place your hands lightly on the forehead with your fingertips touching in the middle.

Wait a moment for you both to quieten down then gently smooth your fingers outwards towards the temples. Do this several times and gradually the tension frown disappears. Then move your hands alternately upwards from just above the nose to the hair line. Keep one hand gently in contact all the time.

Do all this slowly, rhythmically and very softly. If your movements are fast or irregular it conveys a message of anxiety and tension.

When you have finished, your partner should keep eyes closed for a short while to register the feeling of a relaxed forehead so that she can reproduce this feeling herself when she wants to relax. The forehead feels as if it were a little wider and a little higher than before.

When your partner opens her eyes, she should try not to react sharply to

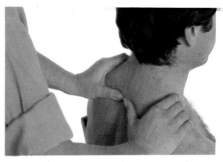

Stand balanced and hold your partner's shoulders firmly, fingers at the front.

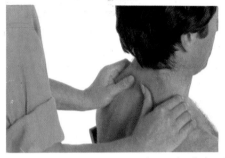

Reach down with your thumbs and roll the muscles firmly upwards.

the light but to keep relaxed.

Finish with gentle stroking this way:

Cup your hands under the ears. With your hand moulding gently to the shape of the neck, smooth down the sides of the neck (this must be very gentle), down the sides of the upper arm and right down to the fingertips. Do this a few times then do a slower stroke to end the session.

These are a few simple massage procedures which you can develop as you go on. Massage for insomnia is described in a later chapter.

Shoulders

Stand behind your partner who sits on a straight-backed chair. Place your hands on top of the shoulders with fingers facing forward. Reach down with your thumbs and firmly roll the skin upwards towards the top. The fingers in front hold firmly so that your partner does not lean forwards, but make sure that your finger tips do not dig in uncomfortably. As you massage, keep the whole side of the thumb in contact, don't dig in with the tips. Your partner will soon give you information about whether you are doing it correctly. You can include some kneading in this position This is shown in the sitting position so that it can be done anywhere. But perhaps it is most effective when lying face downwards.

This massage can be given over clothes and is particularly suitable in class. It causes no embarrassment and most people find that it can be a relaxing and delightful experience.

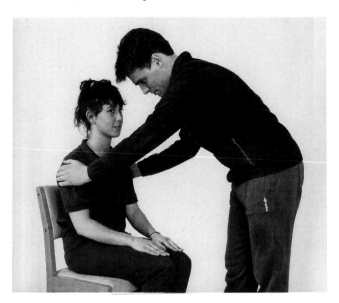

One partner sits on a chair with hands resting on knees. The other stands to one side with one foot forward. He places hands on top of the shoulders.

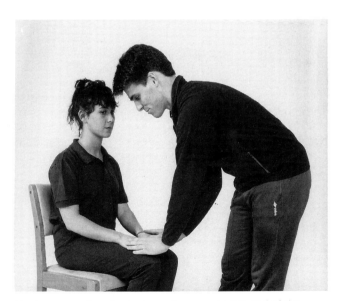

He then smoothes firmly down the arms to the end of the fingertips. Keep this rhythmical, relaxed and unhurried.

81

8 PARENTS AND CHILDREN

The foundations of physical health and the development of personality are laid in the first few years of life. At no other time is the human being so vulnerable to outside influences. From conception onwards, development towards maturity is a process of continual adaptation and re-adaptation to frustrations, upsets and changing life situations. Parents can only hope to provide the kind of environment, both physical and emotional, which will enable the child to achieve his or her unique potential.

Although some of the ability to cope with stress without damaging effects will depend upon genetic make-up, early environmental influences also play a considerable part, and here parents are clearly involved. Parents have a powerful role in the early years in providing the setting for the stable personality to develop, one equipped to adapt to the stresses and strains of normal living.

Before parents feel even more inadequate, let me add that are always second chances throughout life. A harsh beginning may well make for difficulties, but friends, teachers, adolescence, courtship, marriage, even becoming parents can all provide new starting points.

Mothers and babies

Life before birth
Life begins not at birth but as soon as conception occurs, and even though he may only be two weeks old, the child in the womb *reacts*. He or she is a living being from the beginning. The mother's food, her physical condition, drugs, her emotions and fatigue are all factors that are part of the baby's environment. What happens to us physically and emotionally is closely related to the time spent in the mother's womb. It has often been noticed that a woman who is serene and placid, who seems to float through her pregnancy with little emotional upheaval, may well have a child who is calm like his mother. Some of this will be due to inherited factors, but in some part it is due to the peaceful environment provided by the mother in pregnancy.

Can the child be influenced by mother's emotions before birth?
Most pregnant women will hear horror stories, superstitions and old wives' tales about babies who have been born with birth marks because their mother had been frightened by an animal, and other equally apocryphal tales. They have no scientific evidence whatever to support them, and can be dismissed as nonsense. As in much folklore, however, there is an element of truth. There is now considerable evidence to show that a strong emotion experienced by the mother can produce a reaction in the unborn child. Furthermore, scientists are reasonably sure that prolonged emotional disturbance in a mother in pregnancy may sensitise the baby to anxiety and tension when it

is born. The word 'sensitise' is carefully chosen because it does not necessarily follow that the baby *will* be anxious or nervous. The point is that he is liable to be if the conditions after birth tend to create anxiety for the child. Research in by L.W. Sontag at the Fels Research Institute, Ohio, reported on 'the significance of fetal environmental differences' and showed that there is a sharp increase in the activity of the baby in the womb following emotional stress in the mother. He found that when mothers were emotionally disturbed, the body movements of the babies increased by a hundred per cent. This led to babies being born with lower birth weight than usual. Other studies have shown a relationship between a new baby's restlessness and extensive crying and mother's emotional distress.

Earlier in the book I described how emotion gives rise to physical and chemical changes in the body, large enough to be measured. Emotion is subjective; only we can know how we feel. We can neither share the experience completely with anyone else or understand just how someone else is feeling. A pregnant woman is an exception. Unlike other people, she *does* share the physical effects of her emotions, especially the violent ones, with her child. Increase in anxiety or tension causes an increase in the chemicals and hormones circulating in her bloodstream. These are able to cross the placenta and reach the baby. So her feelings of anxiety, especially if they are prolonged and severe, can affect her baby.

All this makes a very good reason for the mother to practise relaxation

Set aside a time for daily relaxation. Later on it will be more comfortable with knees bent and legs fully supported.

during pregnancy, beginning as soon as she knows she has conceived, so that she can help herself and her baby to be peaceful and serene. It is as well to remember though that transient anxiety is inevitable and will do no harm at all. It is the recurring violent and prolonged emotional disturbance that should be avoided. I regret that so many pre-natal classes, which include relaxation, begin so late in pregnancy. When I held classes for pregnant women in a hospital, we found it a distinct advantage to begin as soon as the mother made her first visit to confirm her pregnancy. The classes included information about pregnancy and labour, and discussions to relieve doubts and fears. Relaxation was learnt as early as possible so that it could be used throughout pregnancy at a time when the mother may feel unusual tiredness and emotional sensitivity. After a few sessions mothers practised on their own and returned for reminder sessions nearer the time of birth. The relaxation techniques are not merely for use in labour but to give the baby a calm environment, for mother to use to relieve fatigue and tension, both before and after the baby is born.

Giving birth

Having a baby is probably the greatest athletic experience a woman is likely to experience, but it is an even more profound emotional experience for her, and to a lesser degree for the father. Pre-natal preparation therefore should not merely be preoccupied with the physical aspects but also with the parents' feelings. The very real advantage of a hospital setting is bought at a price. In the zeal for sterility there may be emotional sterility also, and hospitals which use valuable advanced medical techniques may lose sight of the feelings of the mother. There is some evidence that active interference in normal labour detracts from the woman's enjoyment of her baby immediately after birth and with subsequent difficulties in 'bonding'.

The kind of experience a woman has in labour can affect her feelings towards her baby and perhaps towards the father also. A frightened, ignorant, tense mother, with an unhappy lonely experience of labour, or actively managed so that she feels she has no responsibility herself and with feelings of guilt at having lost her control and dignity, may openly reject her baby and resent the father. Other mothers may feel badly about having these feelings and hide them, pretending a love they do not feel, and the rejection is passed on to the baby in the way she handles him. A baby reacts quickly to his or her mother's feelings: it appears to be the quality of handling and touch that the baby recognizes, and if she is jerky, tense, hostile, he is likely to be irritable and restless. (Yes, I know there are many other reasons for baby's crying, but this is one of them.)

In contrast I have had the privilege of being with many mothers who were well prepared and who looked back on labour as a joyous experience. Even when things were not straightforward, and surgical interference was necessary, labour culminated in an experience which satisfied a deep emotional need and which was enjoyed rather than feared. Where fathers were present and were able to help (this is only advised when both partners and the physician wish it) they have always said that the experience was a very moving one and brought the three members of the family closely together in an unforgettable experience. This gives baby a splendid start and helps to provide a good setting for the important first weeks of life.

Skin contact is important, starting from this early age.

Many hospitals and clinics now hold pre-natal classes, and these sometimes involve fathers too. The content of the instruction will vary according to the methods used in the hospital or by the physician involved, but usually they will include different methods of breathing for the various stages of labour, and relaxation. Where the techniques described in this book have been learnt before pregnancy, the mother will have a flying start.

After baby is born

There is usually a reaction of elation, a real 'high' after the birth of a first baby, and you will want to take every opportunity to hold him, caress and fondle him, and it is important that you should do so if it is possible. Some hospitals allow mother to suckle the baby immediately to enhance the 'bonding' process between mother and baby and aid the breastfeeding reflex. The close interaction between the mother and her baby in the first hour

after birth is believed to be important for breastfeeding and the way the mother holds the baby. For this, calm, quiet and privacy are important.

Once your baby has been taken away it will be tempting to stay awake deliberately to savour all the events, relive the excitement and think about the baby. But remember that hospital life is busy and may be noisy and you will be awakened early. It is important that you should sleep when you can, so use your relaxation to calm down and sleep. Use it also at night and during the afternoon rest period. Don't hesitate to cut down the number of visitors if you feel tired.

Post-natal depression

It is quite common for a mother to experience 'baby blues' three or four days after the baby's birth (this is said to be more common in hospital deliveries than when baby is born at home) and to feel weepy for no real reason. For some mothers this is only the anti-climax after a tremendous event, for others it may be sheer lack of sleep, but for a few it may be the result of a sudden drop of hormone levels. In most cases this passes quickly without becoming a problem, but sometimes the physical and psychological reaction to great changes in hormone levels causes more serious depression. This needs expert medical help and understanding from relatives and friends. It is a mistake to try to hide these distressing feelings and no one should be ashamed to seek qualified medical help.

The development of trust and its origins in infancy

The infant becomes aware of the world as a stable, safe and encouraging place if his physical and emotional needs are met dependably and fully. You cannot 'spoil' a very young baby. He begins to know the world as a place to be trusted and in which to feel safe. Once he has this trust he can tolerate the denials that will be inevitable later on. If his needs for food, warmth, comfort and cuddling are not met, his world becomes a frustrating threatening place where no trust is possible and he becomes anxious and afraid.

Mothers and babies need time to tune in to each other in the bonding process. The infant lives in a reciprocal relationship with the mother; she meets his needs, he responds with behaviour designed to elicit affection. He kicks, she responds; he looks into her eyes as he feeds and she warms to him and the quality of her handling subtly changes; he has gestures with hands and legs that convey messages, and later he smiles and gurgles. A recent study of the interaction of young babies and their mothers showed that they responded simultaneously to each other with no time lag in their 'conversation'. This can

only happen when the mother is relaxed and confident enough to trust her feelings and enjoy her baby.

All of us have at times experienced the wordless communication between those who are very close. From the start the baby has a beautifully coordinated set of behaviour patterns which bring out the mother's desire to hold, care and feed him. But she must be relaxed enough to know that her feelings are right, and to enjoy her baby.

When you get home

You are likely to be tired easily at first, and while the hormonal changes are going on you may be more emotional too. Be tolerant with yourself. It is not possible to care for your baby, your husband, and keep up the same household standards you had before. Let the house go for a while. Remember that

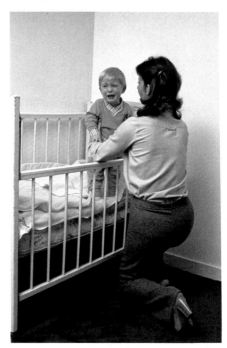

Lift a baby by bending your knees rather than your back.

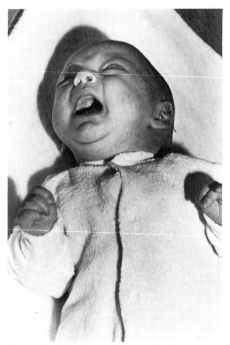

Disturbed nights and days may be a problem.

Hold your baby in a relaxed way when feeding.

nobody copes all the time ... they only look as if they do. A family will thrive on simple basic food and a little dust about if the atmosphere is happy and relaxed. When visitors arrive remember that it is you and the baby they have come to see and not your speckless floor and home-made cookies. I think I am not alone in feeling relieved when I see some natural disorder in someone else's house. It looks lived in and makes me feel less guilty if I am in the same boat when I invite them back. So don't get flustered and apologize. Enjoy their company.

Be careful about the way you lift your baby, especially while your muscles are still vulnerable. Later on, when the baby becomes heavier, you will need to be just as careful.

Bend your knees and keep your back as straight as you can. Hold whatever you are lifting close towards you.

Find time to relax

Deliberately planned relaxation is important now, though you will often feel you are too busy. Find a time in the day that is most suitable for you and keep to it. Don't feel guilty about relaxing; it will help all the family in the end, so enjoy it. Even ten minutes will reduce fatigue and quieten anxieties. Use a kitchen timer if you are afraid of staying too long, but put it far enough away not to be startling.

Relax for a while before you feed baby, either sitting on a comfortable chair or lying with your legs supported.

Hold baby in a relaxed way while you feed him.

Make your household tasks as rhythmical as you can. It helps to work to music, then you can add some postnatal exercises too, especially the contraction of pelvic floor muscles.

Relax on the floor while your children play quietly.

Sleep

All mothers (and many fathers) will experience disturbed nights, and most will adapt quickly to this. Real sleep deprivation, however, can be serious and attempts must be made to remedy this. Some babies are super-charged and cry for more attention than others (most babies are known to cease crying ninety seconds after being picked up) and mothers may become very short of sleep. If this goes on for too long it may cause depression and agitation. Try to catch up in the day if you can, perhaps while baby is sleeping, or go to bed early and don't bother about the night feed until baby wakes for it. Afterwards, relax to get off to sleep quickly. If you have a toddler, it is as well to continue his daytime nap for a while so that you can rest, or at least you could relax while he watches children's television.

Don't build up a sleep debt you cannot repay, or draw too heavily on your energy reserves. If lack of sleep becomes a real problem, don't be ashamed to consult your physician.

Helping children to relax

A calm environment, with parents who are seen to have a warm relationship with each other (even when this includes episodes of anger and making it up) will help the child to feel safe and at ease with the world. In addition to this, the child's basic emotional needs must be considered. These include:

The need for security

The need to give and receive affection

Independence and responsibility

Self-esteem and recognition of his personal worth by parents, teachers and his peers

Play opportunities to develop his physical and mental abilities

Although the above are described as

Wooden soldier Stiff, tense movements.

Floppy puppet Arms and legs all over the place as she relaxes.

the needs of children, they apply to all of us.

Inevitably these emotional needs cannot all be met and there will be times when the child is anxious and afraid. It is worth looking at the list to see where extra support can be given. As he or she grows older and takes more responsibility for their own well-being the child will find relaxation techniques a help.

Relaxation games
There are many game-like activities which will teach older children to recognize the difference between tension and relaxation. At first, use the words: 'floppy', 'stiff', 'limp', 'tight and hard', but later, use the words: 'This is tense,' 'This is relaxed' so that, whenever it is necessary, they can produce the relaxation response immediately they are asked.

Stiff as a board Hold the child firmly to give confidence.

Limp and loose Lifting to test relaxation.

Over to you   The child, stiff and straight, is supported

Past the balance point and she's ready to be caught.

A small push and she's off, knowing there is someone to catch her.

Supported and no fear of falling. Repeat as often as you wish.

Melting ice cream Start off straight as an ice-cream cone.

Beginning to melt . . . arms droop, head starts to drop.

Asthma and breathing difficulties
Relaxation will help children who are wheezy or have asthma, especially when this is sparked off by excitement or anxiety. The child should practise either lying on his back with knees bent, hands resting on top of his tummy, or sitting comfortably in a chair with his back well supported.

Breathe in gently and calmly so that the tummy rises with each in-breath and lowers as the breath is exhaled as slowly as is comfortable. The main point is that there should be almost no movement in the upper chest. It is more fun if a small toy is placed on the tummy which rises and falls with each breath.

If the child kneels, elbows on a low, padded stool, this sometimes helps along an attack when it is combined with the breathing exercise. See that the tummy is not pressing against the stool. It is often a help for the child to know that there is something he can do for himself when he has an attack.

Tense situations
If an injection should be necessary breathing out and relaxing while the needle goes in will diminish discomfort and anxiety.

Older children can apply relaxation techniques to allay examination nerves and to help when they are being interviewed for a job.

Breathing should be quiet and gentle. A few cushions are more comfortable. Asthmatic children should practise breathing calmly. The toy rises and falls at each breath.

Parenthood is not romantic

It is a fallacious and romantic view that the relationship between parents and

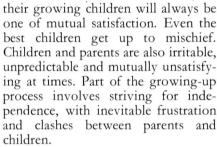
Nearly there. The whole body relaxes, knees start to bend.

Out on the floor. The ice cream has finally melted.

their growing children will always be one of mutual satisfaction. Even the best children get up to mischief. Children and parents are also irritable, unpredictable and mutually unsatisfying at times. Part of the growing-up process involves striving for independence, with inevitable frustration and clashes between parents and children.

For many years I was responsible for a family club, a post-natal follow-up group for mothers who had been in the pre-natal classes. Each weekly session included exercises to help the mothers' figures return to normal, a long spell of relaxation when many tired mothers went off to sleep, then discussion about their families, sharing problems and successes. Many of these caring, loving mothers confessed to having been near battering point with their young children when they themselves were short of sleep, feeling inadequate and threatened as they tried to cope with screaming, rejecting children who did not behave as the books said they should. They felt very guilty about these feelings of hate and rage mixed

up with love and concern, but they found great relief in being able to share their experiences. Talking about it, sharing anxieties, and being able to laugh together released much of the bottled-up tension.

If you are near battering point
If you find yourself overwhelmingly angry and ready to lash out dangerously, *get away from the situation fast*. Use energy by running upstairs two at a time, or do something energetic in the garden for a while. Then use the

Most children fight every now and again; parents sometimes reach battering point too!

emergency STOP! technique (page 66). Say to yourself, aloud if you can, 'STOP' or 'NO'. Then take a deep breath, breathe out *slowly*, relaxing your hands and arms at the same time. Do this again and this time relax your shoulders and face as well. Then breathe calmly and go ahead and cope with the situation, but move and speak a little more slowly than usual. You can then be firm and sort out the problem without danger.

It is as well to practise this STOP! technique at a time when you are not under stress. During a relaxation session, when you feel pleasantly relaxed (but not before), visualize as vividly as you can a situation with the children that normally makes you mad. Keep yourself relaxed and hear yourself using the STOP! technique and then acting in a calm masterful way.

Grandparents can often relieve the pressures on young children and their parents. This is especially true of the relaxed relationships a grandparent may have with a displaced toddler.

The displaced toddler

It helps to understand the special problems of a displaced toddler who is being difficult after the arrival of the new baby. A psychologist once said that it was as if a loved husband had disappeared for a week and then returned with a beautiful, much younger woman on his arm. He told his wife that he had loved her so much that he had gone to get another one and of

Grandparents often have a comforting relationship with their grandchildren.

course they would both love her and look after her for ever. The toddler has the same feelings any loving wife would have, and of course he reacts. No amount of explaining will make him less hurt for a while and some disturbance is normal and must be expected. Adjusting to brothers and sisters is part of growing up and he will eventually come to terms with the situation if he feels he is still loved even when he does show his dislike of the new baby.

94

9 FOR OLDER PEOPLE

It will happen to most of us, probably on a Friday. Fulltime employment will come to an abrupt halt and there will be no more early-morning rush to work. As one pensioner said: 'There isn't a Monday any more.'

Retirement can be one of the most stressful events in life. After the mounting responsibilities and pressures of work which come as the result of age and experience, after the daily organized routine, either supervising or being supervised, the companionship of colleagues, the turmoil of travel, there comes a sudden stop. There is a beginning of what may be twenty more years of living.

For those who have not planned ahead for this change it can be a traumatic experience. Men and women will miss the satisfaction of having a clear purpose in work, they have to face a change in finances, the wife will have more meals to prepare and will find her privacy is invaded. For some there may be an ill-considered change of residence, perhaps amongst strangers. The shock of these unprepared-for changes in life-style may cause a number of bodily reactions. Illness may creep up, not so much because of old age but as the result of a sustained reaction to the stress of a major change.

Others who have planned ahead and are open to new ideas will discover that it can be a most rewarding time of life. They can catch up on many of the interests they were too busy to enjoy before, there is time to enjoy new learning and acquiring new skills, for recapturing and deepening their relationships with others, making new social contacts and for being of service to the community. They may well be as busy as ever, but at things of their own choosing and at their own pace. For many there will be years of feeling fitter than ever now that work pressures have ceased. Retirement needs planning and preparation, but also some flexibility so that new pathways may be explored.

In the calm acceptance of normal ageing and an acknowledgement of the advantages of wisdom and experience there comes a more relaxed attitude to life. This enfolds not only the older person but spreads to those around. An unfussed, uncomplaining grandparent with time to listen can do much to smooth the way of turbulent children, and because they are not emotionally involved in the way that parents are there can be a particularly easy relationship. Older people have a unique contribution to make in lessening the loneliness of others and being available in emergencies. We know now that the saying: 'You can't teach an old dog new tricks' does not apply to humans. Many old people can indeed acquire new skills, absorb new ideas and become enthusiastic about learning. They go at it more slowly perhaps, but more carefully and thoroughly.

Relaxation learnt earlier is a great gift to old age. Not only is it a useful physical skill to apply to living but it brings with it a greater self-knowledge

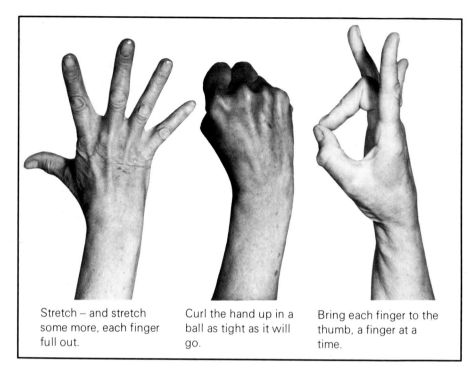

Stretch – and stretch some more, each finger full out.

Curl the hand up in a ball as tight as it will go.

Bring each finger to the thumb, a finger at a time.

which will help to lessen the irritating tensions that disturb relationships and make some elderly people very awkward. It will also aid restorative rest and help in coping with unavoidable aches and pains.

Inevitably there will be physical limitations, but general mobility can be helped by sensible regular exercise, attention to the balance of rest and activity, by careful lifting techniques and by relaxation. Older people need as much activity as they can manage. Swimming is excellent – at least it is something you do with the weight off your feet. Walking is good too especially if it is brisk and you walk tall with arms relaxed. These and other physical activities relieve the tautness in muscles that have been held immobile for long periods, and will help the circulation too. Be sensible though, swallow your pride and only do what you can manage without

strain and don't hesitate to stop as soon as you have had enough.

There are some simple exercises that will help to relieve muscle tension and help mobility. Some of the warming-up and loosening exercises shown earlier in the book (pages 46–63) are useful if they suit you, and in addition you may find these a help:

For your hands
Stretch your fingers out as far as you can. Then curl them up. Do five-finger exercises, one finger of each hand at a time. Then shake your hands loose.

For your knees
Keep your knees mobile by exercising them with the weight off them. Sit on the edge of a strong table and swing your legs gently forwards and backwards in a relaxed way. This is sometimes a help first thing in the morning, sitting on the edge of the bed.

96

Exercise each side of the trunk, shoulder and neck by bending ...

... from side to side. Go as far as is comfortable.

For your back

These exercises are useful to relieve aching from muscle tension and stooping back.

Sit on an upright chair or stool. Place your feet firmly on the ground so that they are beneath your knees. Bend sideways so that your hand reaches downwards. Don't twist or bend forwards, but keep your shoulders facing front. Come up and do the same the other side. Do this smoothly and rhythmically. Don't worry if you feel or hear 'crunches'. So long as they do not really hurt you can ignore them. If there is real pain, however, you should seek some medical advice.

If you are active you can do the bending exercise using the cane. Stand with your feet apart. Bend sideways not forwards.

Use a long garden cane or a light

Swinging the legs is a help for stiff knees.

These exercises relieve tension in the upper back, counteract a round back and expand the chest.

Sit or stand with feet apart, fingertips on shoulders. Stretch up tall before you begin. Turn so that your trunk twists to face one way then the other. Go as far as you can. If you keep your head looking forward you won't feel giddy.

This is a progression. It helps to counteract a round back and takes the weight of your arms off your shoulders. Use a strong cane or a broomhandle. Put it across your back and rest your hands over the ends. Sit or stand tall. Then twist from side to side.

broom handle to take the weight off your arms. Sit tall and twist your trunk so that you face first one side then the other. Close your eyes if you feel giddy and keep your feet firmly on the floor beneath your knees.

Choose your chair carefully

When I was a student at a college of physical education there were long divan-type settees in the library. The Principal encouraged us to rest whenever we could, saying: 'You are very active people. Never stand if you can sit, and never sit if you can lie down.' Then she added: '... until you grow old. Then you should spend as little time lying down as possible, more in sitting, and as much as you can being active.'

Buying a new chair is one of the most important purchases in preparation for retirement. Spend as much time as you can in choosing the one which is just right for you because you will spend a lot of time sitting in it in the future. Try out a number of chairs at a time when you are tired from work or fatigued by shopping. Sit in them and experience the differences. Shift your position several times because no one sits still all the time and you will need squirming room. Take time before you decide. Is it one you will enjoy relaxing in?

Individuals differ so much in length of leg, curve of spine, ease of movement in getting up and down, and there are only a few general rules that apply to everyone. Your feet should easily reach the ground or you will need a footstool. Your back should have good support, especially in the lower curve. It should have a back high enough to support your head and soft arm-rests to support your arms and take the weight off your shoulders and spine. If you have difficulty in getting up and down, however, you will need firm arm-rests. Make sure that the edge of the chair does not reach the soft structures underneath your knees.

An upright chair will be better for those who have difficulty in getting up and down. Use a footstool if the chair is high.

This is wide enough to give 'squirming room' and the footstool will support legs. It is important that it should be as soft as possible so that there is no restriction of circulation. You will probably need a back cushion also.

An upright chair is better if you have difficulty in getting up.

Perfectly relaxed – a comfortable chair and footstool combined.

Sleep

It is often said that old people require less sleep than others. I doubt whether this generalization is correct. I think it likely that old people need as much sleep as before but because of various discomforts they sleep fewer hours at night but make up for it in the day with catnaps and mini-sleeps. It does not matter when or how you sleep if the bits all add up. If you wake in the night, try relaxation first and you will probably go off to sleep again. If you don't, either read or get up and do something useful and promise yourself a snooze in the day to make up. This stops the fretting and worrying and when you return to bed you sleep quietly. There are, however, some old people who spend so much time in the day dozing that they must not be surprised when night-time sleep eludes them. They have already had their quota.

Bereavement

It would be unrealistic if, in considering the stresses of old age, I omitted the greatest one of all, the death of someone who has been near and dear.

Bereavement of this kind, especially when it has involved a long period of nursing, inflicts a great emotional strain which only those who have experienced it can understand. In our culture we have been remiss in ignoring the importance of the period of mourning. Just as we avoid touching one another, we shy away from any expression of grief, abandonment to tears or open distress. But mourning is important and necessary if the sufferer is to come to terms with bereavement.

After the first shock and feelings of unreality the sufferer needs someone who will share in the sorrow and who is not afraid to witness grief; someone who will listen again and again to the circumstances which caused the death, who will be willing to talk about the deceased without embarrassment and is aware of the comfort of a hug or holding hands. Perhaps the need is greatest months further on when kind neighbours cease to call, relatives have gone home and there is difficulty in making social contacts. Every trick should be employed to stop the build-up of anxiety and exhaustion which lead to chronic depression. Adequate mourning and good support from friends will help in restoring interest and a new start to living.

10 STRESS AND THE MENSTRUAL CYCLE

This chapter is about women, written in the hope that it will be read by men. There is no time in a woman's life when she is not subject to the ebb and flow of her hormones. Even in the womb the powerful female hormone, oestrogen, begins to affect the growing foetus, directing it towards becoming a woman; even at the other end of reproductive life when the menstrual periods have ceased she will still be affected by the changing levels of hormones. Perhaps this is why women are often so much more adaptable than men; they have to adjust to the changing physical and emotional symptoms of the menstrual cycle that they have plenty of practice. This was not always the case because, in earlier days, women were either pregnant or lactating so the hormone balance was relatively steady.

The menstrual cycle is initiated by the hypothalamus (which we have seen is responsible for most of the bodily reactions to stress). The two hormones, oestrogen and progesterone, which are manufactured by the ovaries, interact with hormones from the pituitary gland in an intricate and complicated monthly preparation for childbearing.

Many women have little or no discomfort associated with menstruation and accept it as part of their femininity, but others have physical and emotional reactions severe enough to disrupt their lives and cause much distress. The woman may not be neurotic at all; there are well recognized physiological reasons for the disorders.

Pre-menstrual tension

Our understanding of the pre-menstrual syndrome is still in its infancy, but recently the work of Dr Katherina Dalton, author of a number of books on the subject and a practising consultant, has given us more insight into the effects of the menstrual cycle. She describes the pre-menstrual syndrome as the world's commonest disease. There are many women who, as a result of an imbalance of oestrogen and progesterone, combined with over-arousal, tension and fatigue suffer from a regularly occuring group of symptoms. For up to eight days each month, some women experience increased irritability, depression, fatigue and clumsiness, mainly in the few days before the periods begin and perhaps for a day or two after. It has been shown that there is an increased risk of accidents at this time and there is an associated higher crime rate amongst women. There may also be physical changes. Water retention causes an increase in weight and the woman may feel bloated; there may be joint pains, backache and an increase in the incidence of migraine and headaches.

There is medical help available for pre-menstrual tension, but as with all hormonal disorders, at times of stress the symptoms increase in severity. It is for this reason that relaxation techniques have helped those women who do not wish to accept hormone treatment and who do not feel that tranquillizers taken for a long time are the answer to the complications of the menstrual cycle.

If you suffer from pre-menstrual tension you should try to keep a chart of your menstrual periods for six months or so to give you some guide as to when the symptoms are likely to occur. Then anticipate these few days before a period by taking life more easily, dropping inessential tasks and practising relaxation diligently each day. You are likely to feel well and free from these symptoms during the rest of the cycle, so let your hair down then and have a good time to make up.

There are some women, however, especially the excitable ones, whose periods are exasperatingly unpredictable. They may find it worth trying the method of feeling for the pain-trigger areas in the temples and neck which often indicate water retention and tension. This technique is described on pages 116–7 and may give a clue as to when relaxation and a quiet life is especially important.

Some women who have pre-menstrual tension say that they now try to *use* their heightened emotions and harness them creatively when their ups and downs are exaggerated.

Dysmenorrhoea (*painful menstruation*)

Some adolescents and young women suffer spasmodic pain at the beginning of each period. Whereas pre-menstrual tension is said to be associated with high levels of oestrogen, in relation to progesterone, spasmodic dysmenorrhoea is accompanied by high levels of progesterone. So, according to Dr Dalton, those who have the one disorder are unlikely to have the other. Usually the first periods of menstruation are painless. This is before ovulation has occurred but, after that, each period may be accompanied by cramp-like pains in the lower abdomen or sometimes along the inner sides of the thighs. During the spasms, which are not continuous but come in waves, the pain may be severe enough to cause fainting, vomiting and extreme pallor. They resemble labour pains. In severe cases medical help will be necessary but although the basic cause may be hormonal it is known that stress and high levels of arousal are contributory causes.

During the spasms the pain is usually eased by curling up and hugging a hot-water bottle, but in the long run relaxation has been found to be more effective, especially on occasions when the girl is unable to get to bed. She should relax fully and breathe slowly during the first part of the spasm, letting her abdominal muscles relax and rise as she does so. As the wave reaches its height she should breathe a little more quickly and more shallowly, then slowly again as the pain dies away. Self-massage also helps. The flat of the hand moves backwards and forwards across the abdomen, or if the pain is more severe in the back the hand moves up and down the lower part of the spine.

Remember: most emotions are influenced by glands but the opposite applies also: most glands are influenced by emotions. So by learning and applying relaxation techniques you are on the way to exerting some control over these glands.

The menopause

There is a third of a lifetime left for most women after the reproductive cycle has ceased and they will have opportunities to enjoy a 'change of life'. Between the ages of forty-five and fifty-five (though some women begin earlier) the ovaries cease producing mature eggs, grow smaller and stop producing the hormones responsible for reproduction. Because all the endocrine glands in the body interact with each other, when the ovaries cease producing their hormones the others go into action to compensate and maintain balance. The adrenal glands are especially involved. It takes time for full adaptation and sometimes too much of one hormone is produced and sometimes too little. Almost always a balance is achieved eventually but it is the result of temporary imbalance during the adjustment that causes the disturbances that some women experience.

A number of women have no trouble at all; they are the lucky ones whose periods gradually diminish, then cease and that is all there is to it. Others experience symptoms ranging from slight to very severe and these are puzzling and frightening if they are not understood by the woman and by those living with her. These symptoms occur the world over and vary in degree.

The most common symptom is hot flushes. These can be slight and transient, a glow of warmth spreading over the upper part of the chest and face or they can be so severe that the woman is drenched in sweat each time and sleep is disturbed. These are caused by the erratic functioning of the mechanisms which keep the calibre of the blood vessels in close check. These can be quite unpredictable or may be sparked off by slight stress or embarrassment. The woman often feels acutely embarrassed but those around rarely notice unless she draws their attention to it. Before the flush begins there may be feelings of doom and tension, then when it is over there is a general relaxation.

This is a tiresome experience but if she will just accept it (unless the flushes are very severe when she should seek medical help) and wait calmly for the flush to disappear she will find that the reaction is less severe, manageable and not upsetting. When you realize that the adrenal glands are sending out extra adrenalin to compensate for the lack of hormones produced by the ovaries, it is easier to understand some of the feelings and to understand why relaxation will help.

Other symptoms may take the woman by surprise: the sudden whirls of giddiness that seem to come out of the blue are disconcerting to say the least. Provided a check-up has shown there is no other cause there is no need for alarm. This does not last long; it is the anxiety about it that is more upsetting.

Sudden blanks of memory are exasperating. It is not the ordinary forgetfulness we all experience at times but a sudden inability to remember the name of someone we knew well an hour ago. Some women discover that they have lost confidence in their ability and this may be disturbing if she is normally efficient and does not recognize that this is transient and will soon pass.

Fatigue can be overwhelming and unpredictable, coming in waves of exhaustion. This also is temporary and will be relieved if the family take over some of the chores and insist on rest and relaxation periods before she feels too guilty to let up. Perhaps colleagues can discreetly take over some of her work for a while.

Interest in sex does not necessarily diminish after the menopause, indeed many women discover that they have a heightened response, but one of the effects of diminishing hormones is that the vagina becomes dryer and less elastic and vaginal creams are sometimes recommended.

There may also be heightened emotions. Some women find themselves flaring up in a temper over trifles or weepy for no reason and feel very guilty about their reactions. It should all be accepted with good humour by those around and the woman can make it up to them on her good days. It is just bad luck if she has adolescent children coping with their hormonal changes at the same time. If she has severe depression, this is something different; there will be other causes and she should seek help.

Hormone-replacement therapy has become popular in several countries but there are many misgivings about it. Undoubtedly it has helped some women but there will be a number who reject on principle the idea of taking a daily pill for three weeks out of four for many years to come. They would prefer to adjust to the bodily changes naturally, using relaxation to help. They can rest assured that a balance is eventually achieved and there is no reason why, when the menopause is over, the woman should not feel fitter than ever before.

11 RELAXATION FOR DAILY LIVING

The real advantage of practising relaxation comes when it is applied to daily living situations. At first you may wonder whether you are becoming obsessed with noticing whether or not your muscles are relaxed but this is what happens whenever you learn a new skill. After a while you won't have to think about it and it becomes part and parcel of everyday life.

Driving

An aggressive, frustrated driver is a danger to himself and other people. Road accidents are a primary cause of death, but there are other subtle dangers. Aggression releases stress biochemicals, in particular, noradrenalin (the 'kick' hormone associated with the better-known adrenalin). This has a profound effect on the heart and blood vessels. The heart beat of a racing driver can reach 200 a minute and some city drivers come near to this. As there is no opportunity for exercise to burn off the emotion the stress is of a non-productive kind.

An aggressive 'let me be first' attitude shows shoulders contracted and hunched, neck jutting forward and teeth clenched, hands tightly gripping the wheel. This all adds to muscle fatigue and neck strain.

Relax the shoulder muscles, see that the back is well supported, relax jaw and face muscles and use traffic delays to practise slow breathing with the emphasis on the outbreath. The aim is a state of relaxed awareness.

Tenseness when driving only exhausts you and makes driving difficult.

In a traffic jam or at traffic lights practise relaxation.

To relieve neck tension on a long journey, make small circling movements of your head at intervals and then pull your shoulders down as far as you can and at the same time reach up with your head, making a longer neck. Then let the head rest in a good position without strain.

It is the passenger's job to help the driver, not distract him.

If you have had an exacting day, if you are feeling angry or over-excited, or if you know that immediately you return home your partner is likely to pour out the day's problems, relax in a quiet place before you drive away. Even two minutes quietening down will help, but ten minutes will help to renew inner resources.

If you are a passenger, don't nag. It is dangerous. It should be the job of all passengers to keep the driver relaxed and alert, so either bite your tongue, or better still relax yourself. You will be less tired at the end of the journey if you use part of the time to relax. We have found that those who suffer from migraine or tension headaches after long journeys are usually able to eliminate these by deliberately relaxing on the journey and planning for several rest stops on the way.

Children should also learn that the driver must not be distracted. Most parents provide games and activities for them during the journey but if a loud argument breaks out it is worth-while stopping as soon as you can and making it clear that it is a recognized 'rule' that the driver must not have distractions of this kind and that they too must look after the driver.

Shopping and housework

Shopping and exhaustion may go hand in hand. Try to have a break *before* you get really fatigued; use a trolley if you can or share your load evenly between both arms. If you get upper backache when you are shopping, the kind that is usually associated with muscle tension, do the exercises suggested on pages 48–55 *before* you go out. This improves the circulation and the muscles will not get tired so quickly. When you get home relax with your feet up and back supported and don't feel guilty about it: you'll be easier to live with if you are not exhausted.

Make your housework as active and rhythmical as possible. Modern equip-

Non-competitive swimming is relaxing for the disabled as well as the able-bodied.

Parents can easily introduce children to the joys of swimming.

107

patients with high blood pressure has found this a most valuable occasion to use the technique to lower arousal. If you are making the call, relax while you wait for it to be answered; let your free hand go loose and breathe slowly as you relax. When the telephone rings, be aware of the stress reaction (this is quite dramatically shown by biofeedback) and give yourself a moment to quieten down before you answer. Try to keep the tension out of your voice, it always gives you away.

In the office

Try to put aside a time when you can relax either upright in a chair, or resting your head on your arms on a table, or, if you can have fifteen minutes of uninterrupted quiet honoured by your staff, lying flat on the floor. Ten minutes or so will improve your efficiency so it isn't a waste of time.

Social occasions

Some young people are acutely embarrassed at the thought of attending social functions (it is often the nicest people who are shy) and they even avoid the fun of parties by staying

Telephoning often causes tension – be aware of this and practise relaxation.

Relaxation will help if you are nervous of social occasions.

ment is a splendid timesaver but limits movement and activity unless you introduce it deliberately. Plan for ten to twenty minutes' full relaxation during the day.

Telephone

The telephone is often a signal for stress so it makes a useful cue for practising relaxation. A well-known doctor who teaches relaxation to

Relaxing before guests arrive helps you feel calm and confident.

away. They can help themselves by learning how to relax, using calm breathing and relaxing shoulders just before entering and standing tall. A relaxed friendly manner helps everyone else to feel at ease and this makes matters easier. Look to the other person you are meeting and be ready to ask a question, if need be, and to be a good listener.

If you are the hostess, relax for ten minutes before the guests arrive.

Physical skills

Most top-class musicians practise relaxation in some form or other but inappropriate muscle tensions sometimes creep in unobserved. Systematic relaxation practice may isolate these unnecessary tensions and general relaxation controls over-anxiety about performance.

Sport
A measure of aggression and arousal is necessary for some sports but really skilled performers say they reach the stage when, in the 'inner game', they just let it happen in relaxed enjoyment. Undoubtedly recognition of unnecessary muscle tension improves physical skills and full relaxation beforehand helps those who are over-anxious. It is also known to aid in the recovery programmes after strenuous events.

Swimming
Gentle swimming, especially if it is non-competitive and in warm water, is relaxing for the disabled as well as the able bodied. If you are afraid of the water, relax your limbs and control your breathing and let the water do all the supporting.

The age to learn is in early childhood when relaxation and enjoyment of water comes naturally.

All these relaxation techniques can be used in other situations such as being interviewed, or when you are the interviewer; at examinations, public speaking, and any situation which makes you feel tense.

12 INSOMNIA, MIGRAINE AND OTHER CONDITIONS

Insomnia

The drawing by Grizet (right) illustrates the deep relaxation which accompanies natural sleep and the balance between activity and rest required by all living creatures. All animals need sleep, some more than others. Predators sleep long and soundly, those preyed upon have only brief naps and remain vigilant for much of the time. Human beings are rather like this and there are wide differences in the amount of sleep human beings need. Some wake re-refreshed after less than six hours and it would be wasteful to have more; others find that even ten hours is not sufficient. No one knows why, but it appears that good short sleepers are more efficient in the way they sleep and can recharge their batteries in a shorter time than others. It is the quality of the sleep which counts rather than the quantity. Good sleepers have an adequate balance between dreaming sleep (called REM sleep because it is accompanied by rapid eye movements) and the deep non-REM sleep. Both kinds of sleep are necessary and serve different restorative functions.

Most people have times when they sleep badly, usually after a change in circumstances, a different bed, unusual noise, cold, discomfort, exams, but this is temporary and there is no harm in losing one night's sleep. Some people, however, suffer the real horror of long-term insomnia. If you are one of these, you will know that the more exhausted you are, the more aroused you become, too alert to sleep. At night you may be swaying with fati-gue, longing for bed, but the moment your head hits the pillow you are wide awake, buzzing with ideas and unable to abandon vigilance and get to sleep. The deprivation of dreaming is known to cause irritability and sometimes depression. One of the main causes for difficulty in getting off to sleep is anxiety, and early-morning wakening is said to be associated with depression, so it makes good sense to tackle the underlying problems. But often it is just a state of over-alertness and arousal that causes sleeplessness and this is greatly helped by relaxation. There is an added bonus in that teeth grinding during sleep gradually disappears when relaxation is practised.

Have confidence in your ability to sleep

If you are an insomniac you may well believe you are stuck with it for life. Sleeping pills used over a long period are not the answer because, like tranquillizers and excessive alcohol, they diminish dreaming and we now know the importance of this stage of sleep. If you decide to give up sleeping pills, it is important to do this *very* gradually.

Relaxation methods really do work but it requires confidence and some discipline. There will be temporary setbacks because you are naturally an alert person but you can learn from each setback just how much arousal you can tolerate and plan accordingly until you have the sleep problem under your own control and rediscover the delight of a full night's natural sleep.

110

Animals also need sleep.

Check up on physical causes which disturb sleep

Digestion continues during sleep and some foods cause more disturbance than others. A rich meal late at night is asking for trouble, especially if you are excited, worried or tired because this affects digestion. Coffee and tea are well known as stimulants best avoided at night by poor sleepers. Foods which contain substances which are vaso-active (they have an effect on blood vessels in some people) may upset sleep. These include cocoa, cheese, chocolate, red wines. A warm drink before retiring often helps and milk is said to be mildly sedative. A little alcohol helps some but a drunken stupor is quite different from natural sleep.

The right temperature and humidity, a comfortable bed (a firm mattress if you have backache), a dark, quiet room are desirable but are sometimes impossible to obtain. Noise, especially when it is intermittent, can be very disturbing. When you are relaxed you will find that you can more easily sleep through noise, but when

you are short of sleep you may find that the less you have the more sensitised you become to sounds. Ear plugs may help and some people have used a fan heater to cut out disturbing noise.

Good sleepers can ignore a snoring partner, others enjoy it as a welcome reminder of comforting company, but if it causes real distress and insomnia, and disrupts personal relationships it is better to sleep separately for a while. This need not diminish loving, it can even make it more exciting when coming together again will have some of the novelty of courting days.

Lower your daytime arousal

This is the most important of all. It is what happens during the day that affects your sleep. If you are a poor sleeper, one or two planned sessions of relaxation during the day are important. It is too late to leave it until you are in bed with your mind churning with ideas. Daytime distraction in the form of interludes of recreation and hobbies help to give relief from problems. Don't be ashamed to have a daytime nap to catch up on lost sleep. Many famous politicians, generals, scientists and actors have regularly done this to improve their efficiency and to manage with only a few hours' sleep at night. Many people find that it acts as a sedative and helps sound night-time sleep. It takes some of the anxiety out of being awake at night if you know there is a chance to catch up. Good sleepers may not need this but insomniacs can learn to catnap in the day but not later in the evening.

Prepare for drowsiness
Inactivity is the precursor of sleep so slow down your mental and physical activity as bedtime approaches. Avoid any intensive mental work or arguments just before bedtime and unwind in your favourite way. Although daytime exercise is a help in making you feel tired, there is now evidence to show that the old advice to take exercise just before retiring was wrong for poor sleepers (except for sexual activity which, if it is satisfactory, leads a man to sleep though it may leave a woman awake for a while in pleasant reverie). Bedtime routines help drowsiness by reducing alertness so go slowly through your usual undemanding routines. Many people find a moderately hot bath helps them to unwind, but a really hot one is overstimulating. If you read to help yourself to forget your problems, don't use your usual sleeping position for this, save that only for sleeping.

Biofeedback and cassettes
It helps some people to lower arousal by using biofeedback apparatus just before they settle down in bed. Others find a sleep cassette recording keeps troublesome thoughts away but, be-. fore you choose one, listen to several because some people respond better to the authority in a man's voice and

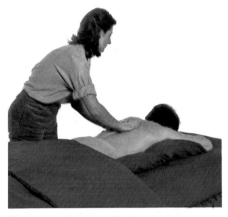

First stage: begin with firm strokes upwards.

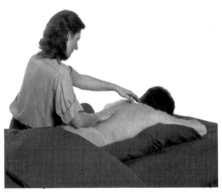

Change to gentle strokes from neck to waist, one hand after the other.

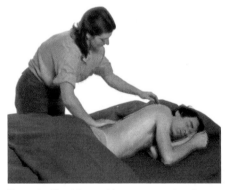

Round off with stroking movements in the sleeping position . . .

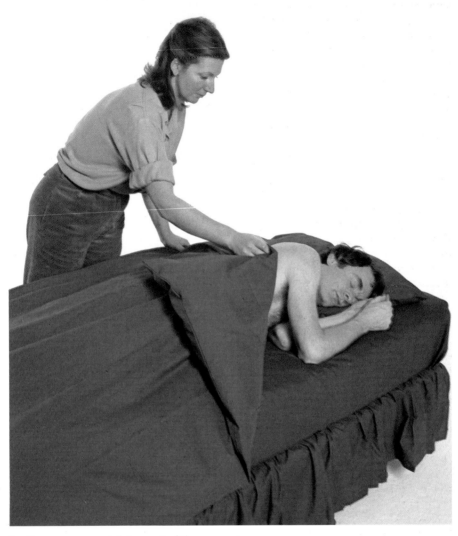

Lastly, cover up and tiptoe out of the room.

others prefer the calming voice of a woman. Eventually you will need none of these aids but will relax on your own.

Relaxation techniques to help sleep
Snuggle down comfortably in bed and begin relaxation with two or three calm, slow breaths, accentuating the outbreath and pausing a moment after it. Begin with your eyes slightly open and during the last slow breath gradually let your eyelids drop. Feel your body sink heavily into the bed. Then relax each part of your body in turn. Don't tense the muscles each time, as some teachers recommend, but just relax them in the way you have learnt, and keep to the same order each time. Don't hurry it and get the sensation of

heaviness and relaxation in each part of the body concerned. If other thoughts interfere, go back to the beginning again and just think about muscles relaxing and the sensation this gives.

If you are particularly edgy, practise the relaxation on your back first, then turn over to your favourite side and repeat the routine in the sleep position.

If you wake in the night

When you wake, relax again at once before you have time to become alert and tackle your problems. Be disciplined and don't allow yourself the indulgence of thinking. It has been said that if you can't sleep it is because you don't really want to. So put tomorrow's problems away, and let go and relax. Don't get angry at whatever woke you because this will release powerful hormones whose task it is to make you alert and ready for action.

If, after twenty minutes or so, you are still awake and not drowsy, don't fight it. Get up and do something instead of fretting. Make a drink, have something to eat or do something useful. Cool off physically so that when you go back to bed it is welcoming and warm. Then do your relaxation routine without feeling anxious and promise yourself an opportunity to catch up in the day or by an early night. Don't panic, because anxiety is the worst enemy of sleep ... it produces the chemicals that keep you awake.

One sleepless night will do no harm. Students anxious before an exam can rest assured that one bad night will not affect mental performance. But try to catch up the next night. Don't get 'hooked' on not-sleeping.

Once you have got the better of your sleeping problem don't let yourself get into the state of continued high arousal that caused it. Once you are sleeping well you can manage with less time sleeping because your sleep is more efficient.

Helping other people to sleep

Help by keeping the atmosphere calm, especially towards bedtime. Massage is a delightful and effective way of helping a partner to settle down to sleep. Mothers know that a child will become drowsy when his head is stroked and the same goes for adults. Some people, however, don't take kindly to hair ruffling so back massage in bed is more appropriate (see photographs pages 112–3).

Your partner should be ready for bed, lying face downwards with a pillow or two under the abdomen to prevent the tension of an arched back.

Stand at the side of the bed if it is a high one, or sit on the side if it is low.

Begin with long, fairly strong effleurage strokes moving from the waist upwards towards the neck and shoulders (see page 79). Move along the sides of the spine first then fan outwards towards the shoulders. Keep the whole of your hand in contact all the time so that the skin rolls in front of your fingers. You can also add some kneading movements. The aim at this stage is that your partner should *feel*, rather than think, so the massage can be quite firm.

After a while change to a different kind of massage. This is soothing, gentle stroking with alternate hands moving *downwards* from the neck and shoulders to the waist. The hands work alternately, one hand in contact all the time, and they are very soft and relaxed, the movement is a gentle lingering one. Gradually make the movements lighter and slower so that even you begin to feel drowsy.

Then let your partner turn over to the sleeping position and continue with a few more stroking movements down the back. Cover him up and go away quietly. It will just be hard luck if you don't get your turn!

Coping with pain

Pain is an unshareable experience and it is difficult to describe to someone else how we feel. It serves a useful function and is a warning that something is wrong and action must be taken. Pain causes anxiety, arousal and muscle tension which make us either withdraw from the situation or keep still so that the injured part is protected. Some pain outlives its original purpose, however, and is useless, or it may be disproportionate to its cause. When this kind of pain becomes continuous it can lead to exhaustion, even a change in personality and depression. Attention is now being drawn towards ways in which the individual can conquer pain by various techniques of blocking the pathways of pain to and from the brain: 'switching off' the message.

Individuals differ in the way they react to pain, some feel it more readily and their threshold to pain is low. The pain threshold is the level at which pain is felt and this varies not only between people but in individuals at different times. We feel pain more if we are tense, unwell, tired, depressed or when we anticipate it with apprehension. On the other hand, it is well known that quite serious injuries can pass unnoticed during sporting events, an emergency or something especially exciting. An excruciating toothache sometimes vanishes as soon as the dental surgery is reached. Some methods of preparation for childbirth are successful in helping mothers to diminish pain in labour.

Anaesthetists are now teaching patients who are about to have an operation how to relax so that they will feel less pain afterwards. Hospitals have also found that patients who can relax require fewer pain-killing drugs, especially when attendants are kind and sympathetic for this is another help in raising the threshold to pain. By relaxing through pain, or by shifting attention from it by attending to another powerful distraction, pain which is chronic can sometimes be wholly manageable, in other cases it helps to diminish the harmful reactions.

Dental treatment

Are you afraid of visiting the dentist? Research has shown that, in dentistry, relaxed patients can tolerate considerably more discomfort than those who are tense. If you are anxious about dental treatment, learn to relax before your next visit. Then before you set out for your appointment, have fifteen minutes of full relaxation. Allow five to ten minutes in the dentist's waiting room and quieten down. Sit well back in your seat, relax and breathe slowly. Close your eyes if you are alone. When you are receiving treatment, pay especial attention to relaxing your hands. Keep your mind on them and let them be loose, floppy and still. Concentrate on this and on calm breathing all the time. If you relax your lips as well it helps the dentist. In addition to relaxation being a help to the patient, dentists themselves are learning to relax because it helps to reduce their fatigue, increases efficiency and a relaxed manner helps the patient.

Headaches

Tension headaches

It is important to see a physician for a diagnosis if you have headache because there are many causes. The commonest form is muscle-contraction headache, called tension headache. It is associated with tension in the muscles of the scalp, forehead and the back of the neck. The headache may last for days or weeks and the sufferer often looks harassed and anxious. One of the

Clench your teeth and feel the ridge of tension which is produced.

causes of tension is clenching the teeth. You can feel the result of this if you do this:

Put your fingers at each side of your head on the temples. Grit your teeth several times and feel the hard ridge of muscle this forms under your fingers. This and tension of the forehead and neck muscles can lead to headache. So muscle relaxation of the forehead and neck will help to prevent this, but general relaxation is even more important. Massage of the forehead and neck is also a help. Remember that many pain-relieving pills have a headache-rebound effect if they are taken over a long period.

Migraine

Migraine is not a modern disorder. Along with epilepsy it is the oldest recorded disease known to man, so modern stresses are not to blame. Nor is it just 'nerves' or an ordinary headache. It is defined as a headache that comes at intervals with complete freedom between attacks and it is accompanied by nausea or vomiting and sometimes by visual disturbances: shimmering blanks and scintillating zigzags moving across the field of vision. It affects twice as many women as men and it can be serious enough to disrupt work and family life.

It appears that the tendancy to migraine is inherited; this is the loading of the gun but it requires a trigger to set off an attack and these trigger factors are surprisingly varied. They include certain foods such as cheese, chocolate,. red wines, fatty foods, citrus fruits. All these contain substances that affect the blood vessels. Fasting can also precipitate an attack. Sufferers are particularly sensitive to bright lights, loud noises, smells, situations and often take criticism very much to heart. Change in any form can act as a trigger: change in weather, holidays, change in sleep patterns, change in hormone levels. Perhaps the most powerful trigger of all is arousal, whether it is caused by something pleasant or unpleasant. All these lower the threshold to migraine for those who have an inborn tendency to it.

Migraine is a disorder of blood vessels and most of these trigger factors influence the constriction and dilation of blood vessels in the head. In particular, the stress hormones (the catecholamines), adrenalin and noradrenalin, have an effect on blood vessels – so relaxation can be helpful in the treatment and prevention of migraine.

At the Birmingham Migraine Clinic in England we have found that many sufferers have learned to control their attacks by lowering their general arousal by relaxation, understanding more about the nature of migraine and the trigger factors, and by being sensible about diet. If attacks should occur, relaxation during the headache is difficult but will decrease the pain and shorten the attack. Massage (fairly strong) of the back of the neck also helps. Some patients have been trained how to feel for the pain-trigger areas in the forehead and neck. In some

Use relaxation techniques to overcome fear of crowds.

people these become especially tender shortly before an attack; steps can then be made to take life more easily, relax when possible and this can sometimes prevent an attack.

Panic feelings

Most of us have phobias about something or other; it may be snakes, spiders, the sight of blood, heights, or it may be of crowds; the feelings of fear may be quite irrational. If you have serious panic feelings which disrupt your life, get help from someone who is qualified. Don't be afraid that you are crazy. Lots of people feel like this so don't try to cope on your own. If you have a mild phobia which is a nuisance, however, tackle it before it gets a hold.

The Australian physician, Dr Claire Weekes, has made a great contribution towards methods of self-help for those suffering from agoraphobia. This is usually defined as 'a fear of open spaces' but she describes it as 'incapacitating anxiety when going a way from a safe place or on being in crowded places'. Her books, cassettes and personal help have augmented medical aid. Her advice is to *accept* the feelings when they occur, to recognize the panic, weakness and fear of collapsing, dry mouth and giddiness as the normal reaction to danger – but which is now inappropriate. Then relax and let the feelings wash over like a wave. Breathe calmly, stay loose instead of tightening up and move slowly; don't rush away. Use the STOP! emergency relaxation technique (page 66) to tide you over. Take the fight out of trying, relax and the feelings will pass. Notice especially the abdominal muscles because when these tighten they induce feelings of panic.

Flying
Many people are afraid to travel by

117

If you are afraid of flying, relax before and during take-off.

plane for work or pleasure even though it is said to be twenty-five times safer than travel by road. If you really want to overcome the fear, begin relaxation training at least four months before the flight. When you have learnt how to let go muscle tension at home, try visualizing the airport and plane while you are well relaxed. Picture yourself calm and confident. Later, if you can, visit the airport, sit in the lounge, look around and relax a little. On the day of the flight practise while you wait to board and, once you are in your seat, put all your attention on relaxing. Breathe calmly and slowly, close your eyes and imagine yourself relaxing in your chair at home. Concentrate on breathing and relaxing your hands. There are many men and women who enjoy flying who had to use these techniques to overcome their fear. Some airlines are now considering having relaxation cassettes for the use of passengers.

Digestive disorders associated with stress

I was first made aware of the value of relaxation for digestive disorders by a professor who had a duodenal ulcer. He was due to have an operation but as there was a three-month waiting list he was advised by his physician to learn to relax. He was an excellent patient and practised daily and used the techniques at work and at home. By the time the operation was due, X-rays showed the beginning of a healing of the ulcer. For many years I have had an annual card from him saying that all is well and he has no trouble. Relaxation has been found particularly helpful in the long-term treatment of dyspepsia. If you have 'nervous indigestion', relax *before* you have a meal and try not to eat if you are angry, tired or worried. Rest and calm down first. Meals should not be accompanied by arguments and strife but should be pleasant occasions.

13 CONCLUSION

There is a growing awareness of the need for individuals to take a greater responsibility for their own health without the excessive use of medication. There have been great advances in community health as the result of improved environmental conditions. Amongst these are clean water, purer food, pest control, better housing and working conditions. But in the field of mental health we have not been so successful. There is an enormous increase in the consumption of tranquillizers and sedatives and in the incidence of diseases associated with stress. Fatigue, mental exhaustion and the effects of prolonged arousal impair efficiency at work and damage relationships with other people.

Positive health is an intermingling of physical, emotional, intellectual and social needs which must to some extent be satisfied. Adequate nutrition, sensible exercise and hygiene are aspects of physical health under our own control. But there is more to health than this because we are social beings and affected by our relationships with other people. Anxiety, anger, frustration, loneliness, joy, stress and tension are almost always concerned with people. Our ability to cope with the stresses of life and to avoid 'people poisoning' will depend on several factors.

Our inherited make-up plays a part but environmental influences are even more important. It is in the early days of life that we first learn to feel secure, to become aware of the world as a place to be enjoyed and trusted. On the other hand we may learn through parental anxiety, constant criticism and inappropriate high expectations about behaviour at home and success at school that we are inadequate and have cause to feel anxious. Even pre-natal influences play a part. So learning to relax makes sense if you are to be a parent. Luckily, human beings are astonishingly resilient and adaptable so there are always second chances even if things went wrong at the start.

Young children can learn the fun way of relaxing and perhaps in the future schools will think it important enough to include in all physical education programmes. Older pupils will need help in recognizing how to apply relaxation to daily living situations to relieve anxiety and fatigue when they have left school.

Adults may find it easier to learn in the company of others. I found that men and women who joined in a group (about twelve we found to be the best number) could more easily release tensions as they learnt together, helped each other and shared experiences about incorporating relaxation into their lives. Massage of the simple kind I have described helped many to enjoy letting their tensions go for a while. There is sometimes a danger in solitary intensive preoccupation with inward-looking methods. The aim of relaxation is to learn a technique that becomes part of active living. A class is not essential, however, and everyone can learn – even from a book.

There are many different ways to find inner calm. The avenue which is right for one individual living in a particular environment may not necessarily be suitable for someone else who is quite different. Prayer, yoga, transcendental meditation, autogenic training (a method of relaxation combined with auto-suggestion), zen, t'ai chi chung (a form of moving meditation which is growing in popularity) are amongst methods which have helped many people. The important thing is that they all gain by being combined with relaxation of the kind I have described. Whatever method is used it must be practised regularly until it is absorbed into your daily life. The aim should be not to withdraw from the world and its problems but to build up resources to enable us to enjoy stress without distress.

We cannot change our genetic make-up, we may not be able to change an unfavourable environment, but we can all learn to modify our reactions to it. Relaxation is a good commonsense way of dealing with the stresses of modern life. If we use it wisely we can gain in self-awareness, and the understanding of body-mind integration, find increased zest and capacity for work, enjoy our relationships with other people and gain some inner quietness and stability in our hectic changing world.

BIBLIOGRAPHY

Stress

Coleman V., *Stress and Your Stomach*, Sheldon Press

Carruthers M., *The Western Way of Death*, Davis Poynter

Dubos R., *Man Adapting*, Yale University Press

Norfolk D., *Executive Stress*, Associated Business Programmes Ltd

Selye H., *The Stress of Life*, McGraw Hill

Speilberger C., *Understanding Stress and Anxiety*, Harper & Row

Wright H.B., *Executive Ease and Disease*, Halstead Press

Methods of Coping

Bahr R., *Good Hands, Massage Techniques for Total Health*, Thorsons

Benson H., *The Relaxation Response*, William Morrow

Brown B., *Stress and the Art of Biofeedback*, Harper & Row

Collick E., *Through Grief, The Bereavement Journey*, Published in association with CRUSE (NB Relaxation for Living also has an excellent leaflet on this subject)

Fink D.H., *Release from Nervous Tension*, Unwin

Gelb M., *Body Learning* Arum Press

Gillett R., *Overcoming Depression*, Dorling Kindersley

Lamplugh Diana, *Beating Aggression, a Practical Guide for Working Women*, Weidenfeld & Nicholson

Le Shan L., *How to Meditate. A Guide to Self Discovery*, Turnstone Publishing

Lipton Sampson, *Conquering Pain*, Macdonald Optima, Positive Health Guides

Mitchell L., *Simple Relaxation*, John Wright

Mitchell L., *Healthy Living over 55*, John Murray

Montague A., *Touching. The Human Significance of the Skin*, Columbia University Press

Rosa K., *Autogenic Training*, Victor Gollancz

Pietroni P., *Holistic Living*, Dent

Rowe D., *Overcoming Depression: the Way out of your Prison*, Routledge & Kegan Paul

Stevens C., *Alexander Technique*, Macdonald Optima

Trickett S., *Coming off Tranquillisers*, Thorsons

Wallace Joe Macdonald, *Stress, A Practical Guide to Coping*, The Crowood Press

Weekes Claire, *Self Help for your Nerves*, Angus & Robertson

Weekes Claire, *More Help for your Nerves*, Angus & Robertson

Relaxation For Living publishes helpful and informative leaflets on many aspects of stress and methods of coping (see page 124 for address).

Parents and children

Bayard R. and Bayard J., *Help! I've Got a Teenager!*, Exley Publications

Gabriel J., *Children Growing Up*, University of London Press

Leach P., *Baby and Child*, Michael Joseph

Leboyer F., *Birth Without Violence*, Fontana

Madders J., *Relax and Be Happy: Techniques for children and young adults*, Unwin Hyman

General conditions

Breton S., *Don't Panic*, Macdonald Optima, Positive Health Guides

Coope J., *The Menopause: Coping with the Change*, Macdonald Optima, Positive Health Guides

Dalton K., *Once a Month*, Fontana

Dalton K., *The Premenstrual Syndrome*, Heinemann Medical Books

Greenwood S., *Menopause the Natural Way*, Macdonald Optima

Harrison M., *Self-help with PMS*, Macdonald Optima

Hilton L., *Easy Does It! A guide to exercise and healthcare for the over 50s*, Macdonald Optima

Melzack R., *The Puzzle of Pain*, Penguin

Priest R., *Anxiety and Depression*, Macdonald Optima, Positive Health Guides

Rose C. and Davies P., *Answers to Migraine*, Macdonald Optima

Sandford C.E., *Enjoy Sex in the Middle Years*, Macdonald Optima, Positive Health Guides

Stoddard A., *The Back: Relief from Pain*, Macdonald Optima, Positive Health Guides

Vines R., *Agoraphobia*, Fontana

Wilkinson M., *Migraine and Headaches*, Macdonald Optima, Positive Health Guides.

USEFUL ADDRESSES

Great Britain

British Migraine Association
178A High Road
Byfleet, Weybridge
Surrey

Centre for Autogenic Training
15 Fitzroy Square
London W1P 5HQ

Gingerbread (for one-parent families)
Minerva Chambers
35 Wellington Street
London WC2E 7BN
01-240 0953

Look After Yourself Courses
LAY Project Centre
Christchurch College
Canterbury
Kent CT11 1QU

Migraine Trust
45 Great Ormond Street
London WC1N 3HD
01-278 2676

Miscarriage Association
18 Stoneybrook Close
West Bretton
Wakefield
West Yorkshire WF4 4TP
0924 85515

National Association for Premenstrual Syndrome
25 Market Street
Guildford
Surrey
0483 572715 (daytime helpline 0483 572806)

National Childbirth Trust
9 Queensborough Terrace
London W2
01-221 3833
(send stamped addressed envelope)

National Council for the Divorced and Separated
13 High Street
Little Shelford
Cambridge CB2 5ES
0623 648297

National Council for One-Parent Families
255 Kentish Town Road
London NW5 2LX
01-267 1361

National Federation of Health and Beauty
PO Box 36
Arundel
West Sussex BN18 0SW

Parents Anonymous
6-9 Manor Gardens
London N7 6LA
01-263 8918

Premenstrual Tension Advisory Service
PO Box 268
Hove
East Sussex
0273 771366

Pre-retirement Association
19 Undine Street
London SW17 8PP
01-767 3854

Phobics' Society
4 Cheltenham Road
Chorlton cum Hardy
Manchester M21 1QN
061-881 1937

Relaxation for Living
29 Burwood Park Road
Waltonon Thames
Surrey KT12 5LH
(sae required)

Samaritans
17 Uxbridge Road
Slough
Berkshire SL1 1SN
Local branches throughout the country. Look in your phone book.

TRANX (Tranquillizer Recovery and New Existence)
17 Peel Road
Wealdstone
Middlesex
01-427 2065

Women's Health Concern
17 Earl's Terrace
London W8
01-602 6669

The Yoga for Health Foundation
Ickwell Bury
Near Biggleswade
Bedfordshire
0767 727271

Australia

Biofeedback Meditation Relaxation Centre
165 Adderton Road
Carlingford
New South Wales 2118

Help Call Service
1A Hamilton Street
Mont Albert
Victoria 3127

Life Line
16 Hamilton Place
Bowen Hills
Queensland 4006

Life Line Centre
210 Pitt Street
Sydney
New South Wales 2000

Parents' Centres Australia
45 Hunter Street
Sydney
New South Wales 2000

Samaritans
60 Bagot Road
Subiaco
Western Australia

Canada

Biofeedback clinics at St Michael's
Hospital and Wellesley Hospital in
Toronto Ontario

**Canadian Co-ordinator of the
International Childbirth Education
Association**
Box 303
Granisle
British Columbia VoJ 1WO

L'Institut International du Stress
(International Institute of Stress)
659 Hilton Street
Montreal
Quebec H2X 1W6

**Lamaze Childbirth Association of
Ontario**
167 Roman Street
Toronto
Ontario

Migraine Foundation
390 Brunswick Street
Toronto
Ontario

Women's Health Education Network
PO Box 1276
Truro
Nova Scotia B2N 5N2

New Zealand

**New Zealand Chiropractors'
Association**
PO Box 2858
Wellington

Register of New Zealand Osteopaths
92 Hurtsmere Road
Takapuna
Auckland

USA

Information on all Lamaze courses
given in the USA is available from the
American Society for
Psychoprophylaxis in Obstetrics,
Washington DC.

**The US Council on Chiropractic
Education**
3209 Ingersoll Avenue
Des Moines
Iowa 50312

Cassettes

By Jane Madders:
Self Help Relaxation (based on this book)
Sleep Well. Help for insomniacs
I Can Relax (for children 4 to 11 years)
Based on the book *Relax and be Happy*
by Jane Madders, Unwin Hyman

By Claire Weekes:
Nervous Fatigue
Hope and Help for your Nerves

These tapes can be obtained from
Relaxation for Living, 29 Burwood
Park Road, Walton on Thames,
Surrey KT12 5LH (send stamped
addressed envelope for information).

Relaxation cassettes and Biofeedback
apparatus can be obtained from Aleph
One, The Old Courthouse, High Street,
Bottisham, Cambridge CB5 9BA,
telephone 0223 811679

Video cassettes (VHS)

A series of six TV programmes on
stress and methods of coping,
presented by Jane Madders can be
obtained from: STRESS (videos), HTV
Enterprises, The Television Centre,
Cardiff CF5 6XJ.

INDEX

126

and sleep 113
testing relaxation of 24
headache
and driving 106
and menstruation 101
migraine 116
and muscle tension 21, 26, 27, 116
relieved by massage 74–9
tension 58, 78, 115, 116, 117
heart 17, 27
and aggression 106
attacks 21
and massage 79
Holmes, Professor 22
hormones 17, 22
affecting women 101–104
alert for action 17
hormone replacement therapy 104
and insomnia 114
and migraine 116
post-natal 86
and stress 16, 43, 106
Human Function Curve 23, 24

insomnia 110–114
and biofeedback apparatus 112
massage for 113, 114
and relaxation techniques 112, 113

Jacobsen, Edmund 31
jaw
clenched 27
and relaxation 58, 68, 105
job stress, tips for 65

knees 70
bent 31, 53, 62, 92
and chairs 37
and lifting a baby 87
exercise for stiffness 96, 97

Leboyer, Dr F. 73
legs
baby's 86
massage for 78
and muscle tension 26
relaxation exercises for 57, 67–70
straight 53

supported 87, 98, 99
life-style 11, 22, 95
Lum, Dr 44

massage 13, 40, 48, 59, 72, 73
for athletes 74
for forehead 74–9
for headaches 116, 117
for legs 78
for neck 74, 75
for partners 77–81
for shoulders 78, 80
meditation 13, 41, 43, 46, 71
transcendental 120
menstruation
disorders 22
and the menopause 102, 103, 104
painful menstruation 102
pre-menstrual tension 101, 102
and stress 101
migraine 116, 117
and driving 106
and head posture 40
and menstruation 101
see also: massage of forehead and neck;
exercises, relaxation
mothers 42, 88, 115
and babies 13, 72, 73, 82–8
and children 13, 15, 17, 72, 78, 114
pregnant 82, 83, 84
teaching relaxation to 13, 93
musicians 11, 31, 57, 61, 109

neck
massage 74–80, 113, 114, 116
muscle tension 26, 27, 28–31, 51
pain 102
posture 35–40
relaxation exercises 56, 58–62,
67–71, 105
Nixon, Dr Peter 22, 23
noradrenalin 105, 116

pain 26, 27, 115, 116
in labour 115
in menstruation 101, 102
and posture 34–40
and relaxation 11
relieved by massage 74–81